Mysteries & Wonders in the Gospel of Mark

MYSTERIES & WONDERS IN THE GOSPEL OF MARK

Shine International

Mysteries & Wonders in the Gospel of Mark

First edition April 2026
Published by Shine International
Phoenix, Arizona
Email: shinebooksmedia@gmail.com
Website: www.shineinternational.org

ISBN 978-1-962580-08-3

NOTE ON THIS EDITION

This book is based on a series of lectures delivered in Arabic in Egypt in 2000.

An earlier edition was published in Arabic in 2001.

For even the Son of Man did not come to be served,
but to serve, and to give His life a ransom for many.

Mark 10:45

CONTENTS

Part I

AN OVERVIEW OF STUDYING SCRIPTURE IN GENERAL AND OUR APPROACH IN THIS STUDY

Studying Scripture has become available to everyone due to the abundance of commentary books and scriptural references, some of which are considered essential because of the type of study they provide and the repute of their authors. What then could this book add? Is this study an attempt to collate information from some well-known sources and present them in a simplified way? Certainly not!

Contrary to the scholastic approach, the material presented in this book has a specific purpose. In order to understand this purpose, we need to be aware of the different approaches of commentary books and scriptural studies:

a. The scholastic approach
b. The scholastic worship approach
c. The worship approach

What is the difference between these approaches?

a. *The scholastic approach* is based on studying some essential references for the book of Scripture that is the subject of the study. Then, the scholar gathers, arranges, explains, and comments on all that he has read in these books, leaving out unnecessary or prolonged explanations and adding comments that further clarify the point or link the book of Scripture with the spiritual life and the Church.

This approach is followed by those who are especially talented in conducting studies and can spare long hours for reading, researching, and studying. They can then select from what they read and rewrite the study for the book of Scripture in a way that suits their audience.

b. *The scholastic worship approach* is based on study and worship together.

Those who adopt this approach have academic talents, together with other gifts of worship and meditating on the Word of God. In following this approach, the person reads Scripture while praying and meditating. Meanwhile, he studies and reads some commentaries on the selected book of Scripture. Studying opens for him new realms and horizons for prayer and meditation. He continues doing so for a while until the final picture is formed before him, and then he starts to formulate it, write it, and present it to the readers.

c. *The worship approach* is based on worshipping God using the Scriptures.

This was a well-known approach for the Early Fathers of the Church,[1] who would spend long hours standing with the Bible open before them on a lectern/reading-stand, reading it in a spirit of prayer and prostrating from time to time as they read, with tears flowing with spiritual warmth. They would pour out their hearts in prayer, asking for the sanctification of their lives and praying for God's people and for the Church of Christ. Such ones who take this approach to prayer and worship receive a revelatory understanding of the book of Scripture they are reading. This is actually a divine gift granted through the work of the Holy Spirit. This revelation that they receive captivates and illuminates them because it is always full of light and mysteries. It touches their souls and leads them to even more worship, abiding in the Lord, loving the Scripture, and rejoicing in worshipping with it.

> *Your words were found, and I ate them, and Your word was to me the joy and rejoicing of my heart* (Jeremiah 15:16).

---

1 Unfortunately, this approach is greatly lacking in our generation.

> *My heart was hot within me; while I was musing, the fire burned. Then I spoke with my tongue* (Psalm 39:3).

The study presented in this book, the spiritual comments it includes, and the revelation presented about the Gospel of Mark are the fruit of this worship approach.

God's gifts are not granted for showing off or merely revealing the mysteries, but are given according to the need of the worshipper and/or the need of those he serves or those who will receive these revelations. The revelation is granted so that it may lead to the salvation and sanctification of the souls by the power of the Word of God and its mystery, and for the glory of God's name in those people.

THE AIMS OF THIS STUDY

There are two main aims behind this kind of study (the study which is the fruit of the worship approach):

a. Dealing with the superficiality which results from negligence in going deep into God's Word
b. Presenting the divine revelation in this Gospel, as it is related to our spiritual needs and the needs of our generation

a. Dealing with the superficiality which results from negligence in going deep into God's Word

We need to grow in spiritual knowledge because its fruits are rich and necessary, as the Apostle says in the following verses:

> *And this I pray, that your love may abound still more and more in* ***knowledge and all discernment****, that you may* ***approve the things that are excellent****, that you may* ***be sincere and without offence*** *till the day of Christ,* ***being filled with the fruits of righteousness*** *which are by Jesus Christ, to the glory and praise of God* (Philippians 1:9–11).

In these verses, we notice that the fruits of spiritual knowledge are:

- To discern or approve what is best
- To be sincere and without offence
- To be filled with the fruits of righteousness

In the Epistle to the Colossians, the Apostle also speaks about the fruits of being filled with the knowledge of God's will, saying:

> *For this reason we also, since the day we heard it, do not cease to pray for you, and to ask* ***that you may be filled with the knowledge of His will*** *in all wisdom and spiritual understanding;* ***that you may walk worthy of the Lord****, fully pleasing Him,* ***being***

> ***fruitful in every good work** and **increasing in the knowledge of God; strengthened with all might,** according to His glorious power, for all **patience and longsuffering with joy; giving thanks** to the Father who has qualified us to be **partakers of the inheritance of the saints** in the light. He has delivered us from the power of darkness and conveyed us into the Kingdom of the Son of His love* (Colossians 1:9–13).

In these verses, we notice that the Apostle highlights the following fruits of being filled with the knowledge of God's will:

- To walk worthy of the Lord
- To be fruitful in every good work
- To grow in the knowledge of God
- To be strengthened with might
- To have patience and longsuffering with joy
- To give thanks to the Father
- To be partakers of the inheritance of the saints

How rich the fruits of spiritual knowledge are and how greatly needed, especially in these days where there is a great deal of superficiality, confusion, spiritual deception, excessive planning, doubt, and queries without answers.

Based on the two references above, we can sum up the fruits of spiritual knowledge and the knowledge of God's will as follows:

- Spiritual discernment, which is necessary and has manifold fruits
- Spiritual growth by avoiding stumbling: in its original meaning, the word used here signifies lifting or taking away all that hinders one's progress in the spiritual path
- Fruits of righteousness: a life that bears manifold fruits

- The fullness of the knowledge of His will: not only knowing His will but knowing His full will (refer to Colossians 1:9; 4:12)
- Living a holy life that pleases the Lord
- Acquiring distinctive characteristics, such as long-suffering, joy, and thanksgiving
- Fellowship with the saints

On one hand, there are numerous blessings stored up for God's people. On the other hand, there is a great deal of superficiality resulting from several factors, such as lack of time, lack of spiritual desire to read the Word of God, and lack of hunger for righteousness and spiritual depth. Therefore, there is a need for a special kind of study that would serve the two aims highlighted above.

To address the superficiality resulting from negligence in going deep into God's Word, it is necessary to present a simple, direct, and spiritual study based on the worship approach that touches the spirit, awakens the heart, and creates hunger in the heart for the Word of God through revealing its mysteries.

In this respect, two methods will be followed in this study:

- *The first method* is to present a condensed background knowledge. Information has been gathered from authentic sources and presented in a simple, clear, and concise way.
- *The second method* is to present the fruit of the worship approach, meaning the special revelation related to the Gospel we are studying. This Gospel study is only one example of this approach, and all future studies of other books of Scripture that will be presented by the author will follow the same steps, which serve specific spiritual aims according to our needs and the needs of our times in general, as we shall see.

b. Presenting the divine revelation of the Gospel of Mark

The purpose of presenting this revelation is to serve our spiritual needs and those of our generation. This revelation is the fruit of the worship approach. Since this is a special revelatory gift with a specific purpose, as explained earlier, the discussion in this study is not a repetition of any well-known commentaries on the Gospel of Mark.

In presenting this revelation, we will follow a certain outline for this Gospel and comment on every section, clarifying the purpose, the fruit, and the spiritual revelation incorporated within the divine lines.

We will also look at the spiritual application of the issues revealed to us through the Holy Scriptures because they were written for our salvation:

> ***For whatever things were written before were written for our learning,*** *that we through the patience and comfort of the Scriptures might have hope* (Romans 15:4).
>
> *And that from childhood* ***you have known the Holy Scriptures, which are able to make you wise for salvation*** *through faith which is in Christ Jesus.* ***All Scripture is given by inspiration of God, and is profitable for doctrine, for reproof, for correction, for instruction*** *in righteousness, that the man of God may be complete, thoroughly equipped for every good work* (2 Timothy 3:15–17).

Part II

A GENERAL INTRODUCTION ABOUT THE GOSPELS

In this part, we will discuss four main points:

1. A brief overview and comparison of the purpose for which each of the four Gospels was written
2. The face of the cherubim and the symbol of each of the four Gospels
3. Christ in the Gospels
4. The Synoptic Gospels and the Gospel of John

1. A BRIEF OVERVIEW AND COMPARISON OF THE PURPOSE FOR WHICH EACH OF THE FOUR GOSPELS WAS WRITTEN

	Matthew	**Mark**	**Luke**	**John**
Written to	The Jews	The Romans	The Greeks	The whole Christian world
Written to highlight	The Messiah, the King	Christ, who conquers Satan	Christ, the friend of mankind	Christ, the incarnate Word of God
Written to clarify that	Christ came to complete the law	Christ came to do wonders	Christ came to save humanity	Christ came to dwell among us
The Gospel's symbol in the different faces of the cherubim	The face of a man	The face of a lion	The face of an ox	The face of an eagle

2. THE FACE OF THE CHERUBIM AND THE SYMBOL OF EACH OF THE FOUR GOSPELS

We will mainly focus here on the view of the Early Fathers of the Church because scholars hold different views on this matter. Some scholars undermine its value, while others ignore it completely.

It is, however, known that the art symbols that we see, especially in early iconography found in monasteries and ancient churches, specify one of the faces of the cherubim for each Gospel, as mentioned in the Book of Ezekiel and the Book of Revelation.

- Apostle Matthew: the face of a human being—one of the faces of the cherubim
- Apostle Mark: the face of a lion—one of the faces of the cherubim
- Apostle Luke: the face of an ox—one of the faces of the cherubim
- Apostle John: the face of an eagle—one of the faces of the cherubim

This is of great value, according to the Early Fathers of the Church. Through their spiritual insight and their eyes that were open to the spiritual world, the Early Fathers of the Church understood that each of the four Evangelists was accompanied by an angelic power from the cherubic order. The purpose of the accompaniment of the cherub was to assist the Evangelist in writing the Gospel he was entrusted, according to God's most high purposes, to write.

It is known that the cherubim are '*full of eyes in front and in back*' (Revelation 4:6). This indicates spiritual knowledge.[2]

---

2 The seraphim are characterised by fire, which indicates fervent praise that is full of love.

This supreme spiritual knowledge was essential in revealing to each of the Evangelists the purpose of writing his Gospel. All the Gospels have one ultimate aim, which is to reveal the Person of Jesus Christ, the Messiah, who was sent for salvation and the completion of redemption through the cross and resurrection. Yet, the Holy Spirit wanted to reveal four facets of the Person of Christ. This is important because the humanity of Christ is abundantly rich. He was incarnated and became man. This incarnation, meaning the humanity that Christ took to save us, had a specific purpose—a different purpose other than completing redemption.

What was this purpose?

The purpose was to reveal a wholesome image of man, according to how God created man from the beginning, and to reveal the richness of the glory of this image, according to God's great wisdom. It was also to reveal God's manifold purposes through this image in which man was created.

These are great, wondrous, and high matters. However, unfortunately, all these matters have been lost and buried after man's fall. This event of the fall happened before man was able to perceive the glory, richness, and wisdom of God in creating him, as well as the diversity of God's image incorporated into the personality of Adam. According to how God created him, Adam was the crown and head of creation. One of the purposes of creating man was that Adam would be *the king and the head of creation,* as is clear in Genesis 1 and 2:

> *Then God said, "Let Us make man in Our image, according to Our likeness; let them have* ***dominion*** *over the fish of the sea, over the birds of the air, and over the cattle, over all the earth and over every creeping thing that creeps on the earth"* (Genesis 1:26).

> *Out of the ground the Lord God formed every beast of the field and every bird of the air, and brought them to Adam to see what he would call them. And whatever Adam called each living creature that was its name. So Adam gave names to all cattle, to the birds of the air, and to every beast of the field. But for Adam there was not found a helper comparable to him* (Genesis 2:19, 20).

Since Adam was the head of creation, he had dominion over all creation and had the authority to give names to each living creature.

This idea is also highlighted in Psalm 8:6:

> *You have made him to have dominion over the works of Your hands; You have put all things under his feet.*

It is apparent here that Adam had dominion over creation; all creation submitted to him and was under his feet.

Adam was also created to be a *priest* for creation. This is clear in some of the early praises of the Church. The worshipper stands before God as a priest, praising and thanking on behalf of the whole creation. This is a priestly act and responsibility. Adam was granted this status and was required to accomplish this role on behalf of creation.

At the same time, Adam had a role as a servant of the Lord to serve God's purpose in creation, for Christ Himself served and is still serving His creation humbly, with self-denial, and with sacrificial love:

> *My Father has been working until now, and I have been working* (John 5:17).

> *For even the Son of Man did not come to be served, but to serve, and to give His life a ransom for many* (Mark 10:45).

Despite being a servant, man was called to partake in the divinity through an indescribable mystery:

> *As His divine power has given to us all things that pertain to life and godliness, through the knowledge of Him who called us by glory and virtue, by which have been given to us exceedingly great and precious promises,* ***that through these you may be partakers of the divine nature,*** *having escaped the corruption that is in the world through lust* (2 Peter 1:3–4).

> *For we are members of His body* (Ephesians 5:30).

> *"For this reason a man shall leave his father and mother and be joined to his wife, and the two shall become one flesh." This is a great mystery, but I speak concerning Christ and the church* (Ephesians 5:31, 32).

This wholesome image of humanity that God originally created and the manifold divine purposes of this image are revealed through the manifold facets of Christ portrayed in the four Gospels:

- **Apostle Matthew reveals the royal and kingly face of humanity that has been lost and distorted by the fall.**

This royal face was originally Adam's face before the fall. Therefore, it is necessary to see this original image, which has become distorted by the fall, as one of the facets of the incarnate Christ so that it may be restored to man and that we may see it and know it. At the same time, it helps us realise that this kingly image is man's original image as created by God because God has always wanted man to be a king. However, God does not want man to be a king according to the fallen picture we have in our minds nowadays, which is often associated with control and arrogance. God has in His mind a completely different picture.

Christ revealed this picture through His life on earth, and this picture was then portrayed by Apostle Matthew in his Gospel. Thus, Apostle Matthew commences his Gospel by saying: '*The book of the genealogy of Jesus Christ, the Son of David, the Son of Abraham*' (Matthew 1:1). This opening of the Gospel highlights Christ's royal kinship to King David.

In this Gospel, we also find the principles of the Kingdom of Heaven and its constitution—the Sermon on the Mount (chapters 5–7). There are also some parables about the Kingdom of Heaven in Matthew 13 and 25. Thus, Christ is given the face of man, a royal or kingly man. He is a King, but He does not control nor oppress human beings like what happens on earth after the fall. Rather, He serves them with the spirit of humanity, meaning as a royal human whose true and original humanity is manifested.

- **Apostle Mark reveals another face of Christ in his Gospel, which is the face of the servant.**

However, again, it is not the servant in the current distorted image, which resulted from the fall, and which demeans the servant as being humiliated and despised and viewed as a symbol of weakness.

Isaiah (40–66) refers to the Messiah sent for salvation as the Lord's suffering Servant.

Throughout his Gospel, Apostle Mark describes the ministry of Christ as *the Servant* who came and emptied Himself to fulfill God's purposes of salvation:

> *Let this mind be in you which was also in Christ Jesus, who, being in the form of God, did not consider it robbery to be equal with God, but* ***made Himself of no reputation, taking the form of a bondservant****, and coming in the likeness of men. And being found*

in appearance as a man, ***He humbled Himself*** *and became obedient to the point of death, even the death of the cross. Therefore God also has highly exalted Him and given Him the name which is above every name, that at the name of Jesus every knee should bow, of those in heaven, and of those on earth, and of those under the earth, and that every tongue should confess that Jesus Christ is Lord, to the glory of God the Father* (Philippians 2:5–11).

In order to reveal the corrected human image of the bondservant in the Person of Christ, Apostle Mark presents Christ as the Servant strengthened with the divine power and who appears as one who is '*mighty to save*' (Isaiah 63:1). Thus, the image of humiliation and belittlement associated with a bondservant is corrected.

Mark was, therefore, given the image of *a lion* among the faces of the cherubim to help us understand that divine power accompanies this Servant (Christ) because He came to fulfill God's purposes.

This is how God willed man, the first Adam, to be when He created him. He wanted man to be a servant, yet without a sense of inferiority, but rather with humility and contrition. This correct and healthy attitude qualifies the person to receive the power of God and His companionship so that his entire ministry may be strengthened with power. Scripture tells us that the Lord dwells with and accompanies those who have a humble and contrite heart:

For thus says the High and Lofty One who inhabits eternity, whose name is Holy: "I dwell in the high and holy place, ***with him who has a contrite and humble spirit,*** *to revive the spirit of the humble, and to revive the heart of the contrite ones"* (Isaiah 57:15).

Through this correct image of the Lord's servant, the work of God's Kingdom is accomplished.

Till they see the Kingdom of God present with power (Mark 9:1).

For the Kingdom of God is not in word but in power (1 Corinthians 4:20).

- **Apostle Luke portrays another face of the faces of humanity, which is the face of the priest who ministers to God on behalf of creation and on behalf of his brethren through sacrifice, worship, love, and gentleness, and with a true and wholesome humanity.**

Thus, Luke begins his Gospel with sacrifices. For example, we first see Zacharias serving as a priest, then in Luke 2, we read about the sacrifices offered in the temple by the parents of Jesus.

Luke's Gospel is also characterised by gentleness and tenderness. He presents Jesus as being tender and as one who has a priestly heart that carries humanity. Jesus is presented as a friend of humanity and one who cares for the various sectors of society: men, women, and children. This is a unique feature of this Gospel.

Luke was thus given the image of *an ox* among the faces of the cherubim because the ox is a well-known biblical reference to sacrifices. Offering sacrifices is the duty of priests and is part of the ministry of priesthood. Though the priesthood ministry was carried out through the offerings of goats and calves in the Old Testament (Hebrews 9:12), in the New Testament it became with *better sacrifices than these* (Hebrews 9:23), where we offer to God a sacrifice of praise, which is the fruit of our lips which confess His name, and do good and share with others (Hebrews 13:15, 16).

> *Not with the blood of goats and calves, but with His own blood He entered the Most Holy Place once for all, having obtained eternal redemption* (Hebrews 9:12).

> *Therefore by Him let us continually offer the sacrifice of praise to God, that is, the fruit of our lips, giving thanks to His name. But do not forget to do good and to share, for with such sacrifices God is well pleased* (Hebrews 13:15, 16).

- **Apostle John reveals the mystery of partaking in the divine nature, which has been granted to humanity.**

This does not mean that human beings become divine or become like God, but it means that humanity has been granted the privilege of being in fellowship with God through a mystery. Our minds might not perceive this mystery fully, yet we need to accept it by faith. We partake of the mystical sacred food—we eat the body of Christ and drink His blood—thus, eternal life flows in us:

> *Whoever eats My flesh and drinks My blood has eternal life, and I will raise him up at the last day. For My flesh is food indeed, and My blood is drink indeed. He who eats My flesh and drinks My blood abides in Me, and I in him. As the living Father sent Me, and I live because of the Father, so he who feeds on Me will live because of Me. This is the bread which came down from heaven—not as your fathers ate the manna, and are dead. He who eats this bread will live forever* (John 6:54–58).

John was thus given the image of *an eagle,* which means that he can soar in the realms of divinity and the heavens. By this, the believer takes his new place in Jesus Christ in the heavenly places:

> *Which He worked in Christ when He raised Him from the dead and seated Him at His right hand* ***in the heavenly places*** (Ephesians 1:20).

> *And raised us up together, and made us sit together* ***in the heavenly places*** *in Christ Jesus* (Ephesians 2:6).

From this brief overview of the facet that each Evangelist portrays in his Gospel, we can see that this profound ministry of revealing the manifold aspects of Christ's personality—which bears within it the corrected humanity according to God's original plan in His first creation, Adam—and its wondrous and diverse manifestations surpass any human knowledge. Therefore, it was necessary that this would be mystically revealed through the help of the ministry of angels who are full of knowledge, the cherubim. Thus, there was this blessed accompaniment of a cherub to each Evangelist.

The cherub was sent to help each Evangelist and to reveal to him one of the faces of Christ. The Evangelist would thus see this face and become absorbed in it. Hence, it would become transfigured before him, and he would be able to outline it in his Gospel.

Though each of the Evangelists revealed the specific face of Christ revealed to him, he did so without straying from the ultimate purpose, which is the completion of redemption. Hence, all the Gospels conclude with the story of salvation and redemption.

It is worth noting here that each specific mystical aspect of Christ's humanity, which He took on in His incarnation for our salvation and which was portrayed by each Evangelist, was harmonious with the personality of each Evangelist.

This shows that divine matters are harmonious and that the Holy Spirit does not ignore or override the personality of the person He uses in ministry. Rather, He calls it to be refined and to discover the fullness of its calling in Jesus Christ!

> *For prophecy never came by the will of man, but holy men of God spoke as they were moved by the Holy Spirit* (2 Peter 1:21).

An Overview and a Brief Background Regarding the Personality of Each Evangelist

• Apostle Matthew had a royal personality.

However, due to the fall and the deviations in the religious concepts at that time, he suffered a great deal from the struggle within him and the rejection of the people around him. Thus, before meeting Jesus, he resorted to tax collection in an attempt to satisfy his royal ego one way or another, for an agent of the Roman Empire was considered to have a distinguished position. Yet, one cannot fulfil God's plan that is inscribed within him without God's grace and salvation. After meeting Jesus, Apostle Matthew discovered this royal personality in Christ and portrayed it in his Gospel after it was practically manifested in his own life first. He found his lost soul in Christ!

• Apostle Mark had a rich, serving personality.

He discovered this aspect in Christ, and his manifold serving energy was released to perform multiple tasks and ministries for the sake of God's Kingdom. It is sufficient that the Bible specifically describes him as *a helper*: '*John* [Mark] *was with them as their helper*' (Acts 13:5, NIV), and as *a minister*: '*Get Mark and bring him with you, for he is useful to me for ministry*' (2 Timothy 4:11).

• Apostle Luke, the physician and artist, had a personality full of tenderness, gentleness, and sensitiveness that was apparent to everyone.

He searched for humanity in the fullness of its meaning, not as the Greeks tried to present it through physiology and art. He might have tried to find satisfaction for his soul that was hungry for the unknown through what the Greeks presented, yet he failed. Finally, he found it in Christ and saw Him in the fullness of His humanity. Thus, he wrote his Gospel to the Greeks, clarifying who Christ is and how in Him alone are realised the fullness of the human being and the satisfaction of the human hunger for the absolute, meaning for truth, beauty, tenderness, gentleness, art, and all that has been granted to man in order to live the fullness of his humanity.

- **Apostle John was hungry for the things above.**

Leaning on the chest of Jesus, he was mystically quenched with divine love, fellowship with the Trinity, and the stream of eternal life. Thus, in his Gospel, he makes us soar high above and takes us with him to what was in the beginning:

> *In the beginning was the Word, and the Word was with God, and the Word was God. He was in the beginning with God. All things were made through Him, and without Him nothing was made that was made. In Him was life, and the life was the light of men. And the light shines in the darkness, and the darkness did not comprehend it* (John 1:1–5).

He wrote clearly and precisely about eternal life in his First Epistle as follows:

> *That which was from the beginning, which we have heard, which we have seen with our eyes, which we have looked upon, and our hands have handled, concerning the Word of life—the life was manifested, and we have seen, and bear witness, and declare to you that eternal life which was with the Father and was manifested to us—that which we have seen and heard we declare to you, that you also may have fellowship with us; and truly our fellowship is with the Father and with His Son Jesus Christ. And these things we write to you that your joy may be full* (1 John 1:1–4).

3. CHRIST IN THE GOSPELS

The Gospels highlight four main points about Christ's ministry:

a. Proclaiming His ministry as the Messiah, the Son of Man, sent for salvation
b. Proclaiming the Kingdom of God
c. Proclaiming the love of the Father
d. Proclaiming salvation based on the grace of redemption

We notice that Christ had hidden the fact that He was the Messiah sent for salvation until towards the end of His ministry. Then, He wanted to reveal this matter only to His disciples; thus, He asked them: *'Who do men say that I, the Son of Man, am?'* (Matthew 16:13). This truth was to become known to everyone through the resurrection and the pouring of the Holy Spirit: *'No one can say Jesus is Lord except by the Holy Spirit'* (1 Corinthians 12:3).

Thus, unless we experience the power of resurrection and the outpouring of the Day of Pentecost, our partaking in the divine nature will remain inactive, and the revelation of the truth of His divinity will remain veiled as well.

4. THE SYNOPTIC GOSPELS VERSUS THE GOSPEL OF APOSTLE JOHN

Scholars refer to the Gospels of Apostles Matthew, Mark, and Luke as the Synoptic Gospels, meaning they are similar, whereas the Gospel of Apostle John is considered unique regarding its approach and its order of events.

The three Synoptic Gospels aim to reveal that Christ's rich personality, with its different facets, reflects the corrected image of creation before the fall in its amazing and manifold manifestations.

Therefore, each of these Evangelists focused mainly on the aim set before him, which was to reveal the particular image of Christ that he was called to reveal. Each Evangelist focused on making this image of Christ apparent through his Gospel to the extent that he disregarded the chronological order of events (except for Mark because he wrote to the Romans, who cared about time sequence).

Each of the three Apostles gathered all the events that would aid in revealing the facet of Christ they wanted to highlight, without considering the chronological order, and put these events together in a paragraph or a chapter. Then, they would move on to another part of the image where they would also gather and present all events, sayings, and deeds of Christ's life related to it regardless of the chronological order, and so on. By this, the image and the message that were meant to be highlighted from the life of the Messiah were revealed through the Gospel. Then, at the end of the Gospel, they all mentioned the story of redemption as it is considered the crown and the ultimate aim of the Messiah's ministry.

Since this image can only be revealed through the sayings and deeds of Christ, the emphasis in the three Gospels is on the second and third years[3] of Christ's ministry because these two years comprise the majority of Christ's deeds and sayings. This led them to be brief in recording the events of the first year of Christ's ministry and the final six months of His ministry. Those of the first are recorded in a few verses in the first chapter of each of the three Synoptic Gospels, and those of the latter are also recorded in a few verses mentioned before the story of the crucifixion and resurrection.

Therefore, these Gospels are considered synoptic in that they serve the aim of revealing the wholesome humanity of Christ, the Messiah, and the act of redemption which He completed, focusing on the events of the second and third years of Christ's ministry.

Apostle John, on the other hand, took another approach in outlining his Gospel. His aim was not to reveal the wholesome humanity of Christ but rather to reveal Christ's divine humanity, meaning God who became man, was incarnated for us, and *'made His dwelling among us'* (John 1:14, NIV) or *set His tent among us,*[4] according to the original translation.

Thus, Apostle John concluded his Gospel, saying:

> *And truly Jesus did many other signs in the presence of His disciples, which are not written in this book; but these are written* ***that you may believe that Jesus is the Christ, the Son of God*** (John 20:30, 31a).

To highlight his aim in focusing on this theme, he continued, saying: *'And that believing you may have life in His name'* (John 20:31b).

---

3 Christ's ministry lasted three and a half years.
4 See G4637 in Strong's Greek Lexicon.

He emphasised the same point in his First Epistle because this aim was the subject of his concern due to its importance:

> *These things I have written to you who believe in the name of the Son of God,* ***that you may know that you have eternal life,*** *and that you may continue to believe in the name of the Son of God. Now this is the confidence that we have in Him, that if we ask anything according to His will, He hears us. And if we know that He hears us, whatever we ask, we know that we have the petitions that we have asked of Him* (1 John 5:13–15).

He was also preoccupied with recording the events that occurred during the first year and last six months of Christ's ministry, as these periods were hardly mentioned in the other Gospels.[5] This was, of course, through the inspiration of the Holy Spirit to reveal everything related to the ministry of the Lord.

Thus, at the beginning of his Gospel, Apostle John set apart five chapters for the first year of Christ's ministry, mentioning the most important events and their significance. After each event or ministry, he wrote a comment or teaching related to it in order to highlight the complete divine meaning of the event or situation.

He also recorded the last six months of Christ's ministry in about six chapters (chapters 7–12), beginning with the last Feast of Tabernacles till the last week, the week of the Lord's suffering (the Passion Week). By this, he kept only one chapter (chapter 6) for the events related to the second and third years of Christ's ministry because everything related to this period had already been recorded in detail in the other Gospels. He only chose the event of feeding the five thousand and linked it with the teachings

5 Apostle John wrote his Gospel towards the end of the first century, whereas the Synoptic Gospels were written much earlier. Therefore, most likely, Apostle John had an idea about the content of the Synoptic Gospels, as some resources state; hence, in writing his Gospel, he included the events that were not included in the other Gospels.

and deeds of Christ mentioned in his Gospel so that it would be in harmony with the general purpose of the Gospel, which is eternal life—since the story of feeding the five thousand is directly related to Jesus presenting Himself as the living bread, the food of eternal life.

We also see that Apostle John is the only Apostle who mentioned the events of the last days of Christ, meaning the Last Supper and the Sunday of the Resurrection, in great detail, dedicating nine chapters (chapters 13–21) to them. In these chapters, we see the Lord taking His disciples alone to the Upper Room, comforting, teaching, and preparing them for the coming events—the events of the crucifixion. Therefore, John wrote the chapters of the Paraclete[6] (14–16). He is the only Apostle who recorded them.

---

6 A Greek word that means *the Holy Spirit, the Comforter.*
Mullins, E. "Paraclete - International Standard Bible Encyclopaedia." Blue Letter Bible. Last Modified May 5, 2003.

Part III

THE GOSPEL OF MARK THE EVANGELIST

When studying any book of Scripture, we need to know some essential context and background of the book of Scripture that we are studying so that we may understand the verses more clearly. This includes knowing about the writer, the date of writing, to whom it was written, the main subject, etcetera. This background is important if we want to enter into the depths of the message of the book of Scripture.

Therefore, in this section, we will discuss the following main points as a background of the Gospel and its writer before beginning the detailed study of the Gospel itself:

1. The Birth and Upbringing of Apostle Mark
2. Apostle Mark's Ministry After the Day of Pentecost
3. Apostle Mark's Ministry in Libya (Pentapolis), Egypt, and Other Countries[7]
4. Characteristics of the Gospel of Mark
5. Christ in the Gospel of Mark
6. Outline of the Gospel of Mark

However, it is important to note here that we are not discussing these points merely to know some background information or history, as one may in an intellectual or a scholastic approach; rather, in this context, we need to learn an important principle, based on the mind of the Early Fathers of the Church, for studying any book of Scripture.

When studying a book of Scripture, we ought to know the personality and characteristics of its writer through all that is mentioned about him in the Scriptures (and sometimes through what has been handed down). When reading any book of Scripture, the Early Fathers of the Church made sure to get acquainted with its

---

7 He also evangelised in Rome with Apostle Peter, in the Adriatic region, and in Colossae (Colossians 4:10, 11).

writer. For example, when they would read the Book of Jeremiah, they would continue to learn characteristics mentioned about Jeremiah in his Book until they reached a point where they would truly know the writer, as if they could see him before their eyes. This enabled them to more greatly comprehend what this writer had written to the generations in his prophetic book. They would do the same with every book of Scripture and its writer because it is written: *'For prophecy never came by the will of man, but holy men of God spoke as they were moved by the Holy Spirit'* (2 Peter 1:21). Unfortunately, this experience has become almost absent in the Church today, and some may even consider it difficult to comprehend.

1. THE BIRTH AND UPBRINGING OF APOSTLE MARK

Apostle Mark was born in Cyrene,[8] which was part of Libya at that time (one of the five Greek cities in North Africa). He was from the tribe of Levi, a family of priests. His parents were Jewish and were interested in religious matters. His parents were called Aristobulus and Miriam.

He came from a rich and politically influential family who had the privilege of joining the Roman Senate because it was among the families that helped Caesar in his political and military efforts. These political privileges granted to Mark's family had an influence on his life and ministry,[9] as they made certain things feasible for him that were not feasible for other disciples, such as having the ability to follow the Lord's trial. Parts of the trial were in the Roman language, and hence could only be understood by observers who knew the language.

Apostle Mark was also highly educated. This was reflected in his linguistic abilities. He mastered three languages: Hebrew, Greek, and Latin. The Hebrew language was his mother tongue and the language of his religion. The Greek language was associated with international civilisation at the time, and it was taught to the children of elite and rich families. He also knew Latin because his family had membership in the Roman Senate.

This background and these skills gave him the privilege of being able to closely follow everything that took place in the Lord's trial. This influenced his life, thoughts, writing, and Gospel. Hence, we also see that this is the only Gospel among the three Synoptic

8 Modern day Shahhat, Libya
9 God, in His wisdom, plans all that concerns the ministry of His Kingdom in a special way.

Gospels that allocated six chapters to the story of the Lord's Passion, beginning from Christ entering Jerusalem to His resurrection. The other Gospels, on the other hand, each allocated only three chapters to these events. These six chapters of the Gospel of Mark actually constitute more than one-third of his Gospel, which consists of 16 chapters, whereas the three chapters in the other Gospels that speak about the Passion of Christ constitute only around one-eighth to one-ninth of each Gospel.

We should also not forget Apostle Mark's considerate and tender personality. His Hebrew name was *John* which means *God is compassionate and merciful.* This name reveals aspects of his personality because, according to the Jewish tradition, the choice of one's name reveals aspects of one's personality.

This compassionate and highly educated personality was also broad, rich, and gifted. He is the disciple who was able to journey to many countries to minister and was able to adapt to different nationalities in these countries because of his distinct education, his inner broadness, and his broad mind. He was also able to closely accompany two great Apostles, Peter and Paul,[10] in some of the stages of their lives and ministries, and was able himself to have various and diverse ministries. He was *a helper, a teacher, an Evangelist, an Apostle,* and *an author of one of the Gospels.*

His family moved to Jerusalem after the Berber persecution and attacks on Libya. They lived in the Jewish capital,[11] where they bought a house and an olive grove with an oil press to work in. This house is the one referred to in some places in Scripture as *'the house of Mary, the mother of John whose surname was Mark'* (Acts 12:12).

10 1 Peter 5:13; 2 Timothy 4:11
11 This is because they adored religious matters and could financially afford to live there.

From history, we know that it is the house the Lord visited with His disciples and in which Jesus washed the disciples' feet, celebrated the Passover feast, and instituted the sacrament of the Eucharist. Also, the disciples met in this house after the crucifixion and resurrection for prayer. It is *the Upper Room* referred to in the Gospels. It is the place where the Holy Spirit came upon the disciples on the Day of Pentecost.

As for the grove, it is the grove of the oil press, which is Gethsemane,[12] where the Lord often met with His disciples (see John 18:2) because it was a secluded place suitable for prayer, meditation, and private talks between the Lord and His disciples away from the crowds of people.

It is said that Apostle Mark was around 15–18 years old when his family moved from Libya to Jerusalem. This means that from early on he was given the chance to follow all the events, sayings, and deeds of the Lord, especially that the Lord often visited the house of Mark's family.

According to history/historical accounts, Apostle Mark is one of the Seventy Disciples whom the Lord appointed to be sent forth (see Luke 10:1). His Hebrew name is *John,* which means *God is compassionate and merciful.* His Greek name is *Mark,* which means *heavy hammer.* It was common among rich, educated families whose children had learned Greek to give their children Greek names in addition to their Hebrew names in order to use these names when they would travel in the Greek world.

The meaning of the Greek name given to him draws our attention. It must have been God's plan for him. It means *heavy hammer,* that is, *sledgehammer,* and this actually refers to the type of his ministry and Gospel.

---

12 Gethsemane literally means *oil press.*

So, if the name *John* reveals the type of his personality, the name *Mark* reveals the type of his ministry because he wrote the Gospel containing the message of God's Kingdom which was appointed to him in a highly precise way, yet in a way full of power. It is a Gospel that reveals Jesus, the Servant of the Lord, who is strengthened by God's power and accompanied by the cherub of power, the lion. Thus, the words of his Gospel, which are precise and goal-oriented, are like a sledgehammer, bearing within them the mystery of the power of the Holy Spirit. This sledgehammer banged strongly on the hearts to awaken them and change them from one state, which was the corruption of the world at that time, to the opposite state, which was to belong to the Kingdom of God proclaimed with power in the Apostolic Age. This is the mystery of the Gospel written by Apostle Mark. This mystery is preserved in the Gospel throughout all ages. Whenever the mystery of this Gospel is opened for us by the power of the Holy Spirit, we experience the effect and mystery of the sledgehammer and witness its fruits in our ministry.

2. APOSTLE MARK'S MINISTRY AFTER THE DAY OF PENTECOST

We mentioned that the house of Apostle Mark is the place where the Holy Spirit was poured out on the disciples on the Day of Pentecost. Thus, Mark was present with the disciples and received the grace of the Comforter with them. After that, his ministries and missions began, which we can deduce from the Book of Acts and from the accounts handed down to us.

The first thing we read about Apostle Mark in the Book of Acts is in Acts 12:25:

> *And Barnabas and Saul returned from Jerusalem when they had fulfilled their ministry, and they also took with them John whose surname was Mark.*

From this, we deduce that together with Saul (Paul) and Barnabas, Mark took part in the ministry of distributing gifts collected in Antioch to the poor in Jerusalem during the famine referred to in Acts 11:27–30.

Apostle Mark accompanied Apostles Paul and Barnabas on their first mission (Acts 13:1–3):

> *The two of them* [Barnabas and Paul], *sent on their way by the Holy Spirit, went down to Seleucia and sailed from there to Cyprus. When they arrived at Salamis, they proclaimed the word of God in the Jewish synagogues. John* [Mark] *was with them as their helper* (Acts 13:4, 5, NIV).

According to the original language and the historical accounts handed down about Apostle Mark's ministry with Apostles Peter and Paul,[13] the word *helper* here indicates that he sometimes

13 Apostle Mark also helped Apostle Peter in his ministry, as we will shortly highlight.

worked with them as a translator and interpreter of the Holy Scriptures due to his linguistic abilities and educational knowledge.

According to the original language, the word also means *a schoolteacher*. Since Apostle Mark was from a priestly origin (the tribe of Levi), knew the rituals, and was accustomed to the idea of handing them down due to his Jewish religious background, he was responsible for teaching and preparing the catechumens. The catechumens were those who believed in Jesus Christ through the evangelism of the two Apostles and needed to be prepared through knowledge, teaching, and handing down in order to receive baptism and join the Church. This skill enabled Apostle Mark to lay down the foundation of faith and offer believers the teaching they needed, as we shall see shortly.

We later read that he did not complete the first journey with the two Apostles, Barnabas and Paul, and he returned to Jerusalem:

> *Now when Paul and his party set sail from Paphos, they came to Perga in Pamphylia; and John* [Mark], *departing from them, returned to Jerusalem* (Acts 13:13).

However, in Acts 15, which speaks about the first council held in Jerusalem, it is apparent that Mark was present at the council with the two Apostles as he was in Jerusalem at that time.

A disagreement occurred between Paul and Barnabas about whether or not to take Mark with them on their first visit back to see the brethren whom they had preached to on their first journey:

> *Then after some days Paul said to Barnabas, "Let us now go back and visit our brethren in every city where we have preached the word of the Lord, and see how they are doing." Now Barnabas was determined to take with them John called Mark. But Paul insisted that they should not take with them the one who had departed from them in Pamphylia, and had not gone with them*

to the work. Then the contention became so sharp that they parted from one another. And so Barnabas[14] *took Mark and sailed to Cyprus; but Paul chose Silas and departed, being commended by the brethren to the grace of God* (Acts 15:36–40).

Later, we will discuss the ministry of Apostle Mark in Cyprus according to what we know from history and what was handed down, but now we want to follow his ministry according to the Book of Acts.

We notice that after the disagreement mentioned in Acts 15, Mark's name is not mentioned again in the Book of Acts. This covers a period of about 10 years—the period of his ministry in Egypt and Libya. Then, he is mentioned again in the Epistles:

Aristarchus my fellow prisoner greets you, with Mark the cousin of Barnabas (about whom you received instructions: if he comes to you, welcome him) (Colossians 4:10).

As do Mark, Aristarchus, Demas, Luke, my fellow labourers (Philemon 24).

Only Luke is with me. Get Mark and bring him with you, for he is useful to me for ministry (2 Timothy 4:11).

Thus, Mark returned to help Apostle Paul after the first separation in Acts 15:36–40. Apostle Paul testified that he was helpful to him in his ministry.

Mark is also mentioned in the First Epistle of Peter:

She who is in Babylon, elect together with you, greets you; and so does Mark my son (1 Peter 5:13).

---

14 Mark was the cousin of Barnabas (Colossians 4:10). Other translations state that he was his nephew (Colossians 4:10, Arabic Bible, Van Dyke Version).

This verse shows that he helped Apostle Peter in his ministry and highlights the spiritual intimacy between the two Apostles, expressed in Apostle Peter saying *my son Mark*.

A Comment

We may wonder why Apostle Barnabas chose to accompany Mark, leaving the company of Apostle Paul. This was not because of the kinship between Mark and Barnabas, as one may initially think, but because this was part of Apostle Barnabas' specific calling. The name *Barnabas* means *Son of Encouragement*:

> *And Joses, who was also named Barnabas by the Apostles (which is translated Son of Encouragement), a Levite of the country of Cyprus* (Acts 4:36).

The phrase *Son of Encouragement* highlights that he had a ministry of encouragement, that is, a special anointing to encourage souls undergoing specific circumstances that required encouragement. This is apparent in the conduct of Barnabas towards Saul (Apostle Paul) on more than one occasion, as we read in the Book of Acts:

> *And when Saul had come to Jerusalem, he tried to join the disciples; but they were all afraid of him, and did not believe that he was a disciple. But Barnabas took him and brought him to the apostles. And he declared to them how he had seen the Lord on the road, and that He had spoken to him, and how he had preached boldly at Damascus in the name of Jesus. So he was with them at Jerusalem, coming in and going out* (Acts 9:26–28).

Here we see Barnabas' encouraging role until Saul was accepted by the Apostles and was able to move about freely with them and even share in the ministry: *'And he* [Apostle Paul] *spoke boldly in the name of the Lord Jesus'* (Acts 9:29).

On another occasion, we read:

> *Then Barnabas departed for Tarsus to seek Saul. And when he had found him, he brought him to Antioch. So it was that for a whole year they assembled with the church and taught a great many people. And the disciples were first called Christians in Antioch* (Acts 11:25, 26).

Again, Barnabas brought Saul back from his seclusion and his ministry in his own land of Tarsus, to Antioch which was later considered a center for ministering to the Gentiles—a ministry that Apostle Paul was set apart for. This was done through clear and specific guidance of the Holy Spirit to the Son of Encouragement, Barnabas, to bring the Apostle of the Gentiles to the center of his ministry (before it was proclaimed in Acts 13:1–3). Thus, for one whole year, they laid down the foundation for ministering to the Gentiles in Antioch together.

After Apostle Paul's ministry was manifested and Barnabas had accompanied him on his first journey, it was time for Barnabas to encourage and support another Apostle, Mark. Thus, he took him with him to Cyprus, Barnabas' country of origin, to support him in his ministry until his mission was manifested.

3. EVANGELISING IN LIBYA (PENTAPOLIS), EGYPT, AND OTHER COUNTRIES[15]

This period is not mentioned in the Book of Acts, but its events were preserved through authentic accounts, which were verbally passed on from generation to generation in the Church of Egypt. Due to severe persecution, it was not possible for the old manuscripts to be preserved, as many of them were stolen, burned, or lost during the difficult times that the Church of Egypt underwent over many centuries. However, verbal handing down was strong among the believers of Egypt.

This period spans 10 years and comprises Apostle Mark's ministry in Egypt and Libya. It can be summed up as follows:

a. Apostle Mark's Ministry with Apostle Peter
b. Apostle Mark's Ministry with Apostle Barnabas

a. Apostle Mark's Ministry with Apostle Peter

This was after Apostle Peter came out of prison and escaped to Antioch.

From Antioch, the two Apostles went to Egypt, where there was a large group of Jews. We know that the ministry of Apostle Peter was among the scattered Jews, as made clear in his First Epistle (1 Peter 1:1). It was there that he wrote his First Epistle (1 Peter 5:13).[16] The two Apostles preached the gospel in Old Cairo, then in the Oasis. After that, Apostle Mark went to Alexandria, while Apostle Peter returned to Antioch.

15 Resources used in collating the events of the Apostle's ministry in Egypt include: *The Prologue of Ohrid* by St. Nikolai Velimirovic and the Coptic Orthodox Synaxarium (Book of the Lives of the Saints).

16 According to many scholars, Babylon mentioned here is considered Old Cairo.

b. Apostle Mark's Ministry with Apostle Barnabas

After leaving Jerusalem (Acts 15:36), Apostle Mark went with Apostle Barnabas to Cyprus, then to Libya, Egypt, and Alexandria.

History[17] and the accounts passed on by the believers reveal that the events went as follows:

After leaving Cyprus, Mark spent two years in the five Greek cities (Pentapolis) where many Jewish people lived. He proclaimed the gospel of Christ there. Many miracles took place, and a great number of people, about 5000, as some accounts say, believed in Christ. From there, he went to Alexandria, where he spent seven years.

When the Apostle entered the city of Alexandria, his shoe was torn because of the amount he had walked during his preaching and evangelism. He went to a cobbler in the city, called Anianus, to repair it. While Anianus was repairing the shoe, the awl pierced his finger. Anianus shouted in Greek, saying, 'Heis ho Theos!' which means, *O, one God!* When Apostle Mark heard these words, he found it suitable to talk to him about the one God. The Apostle took some clay, spat on it, and applied it to Anianus' finger, saying, 'In the Name of Jesus Christ, the Son of God,' and the wound healed immediately, as if nothing had happened to his finger. Astonished at this miracle, the cobbler invited Mark to his home. Hearing Mark's preaching, Anianus was baptised, along with his entire household.

---

17 Butler, Alban. The Lives of the Fathers, Martyrs, and Other Principal Saints. J. Chambers, 1756.

Eusebius, Bishop Of Caesarea. Ecclesiastical History. Translated by Kirsopp Lake., D.D., D.Litt, Volume 1, William Heinemann, 1926, Book II, Chapter 16.

Eusebius, Bishop of Caesarea. Nicene and Post-Nicene Fathers. Translated by Philip Schaff and Henry Wace, Series II, Volume I, Christian Literature Company, 1 June 2007.

Ibn Al-Muqaffa', Severus, Bishop of Al-Ashmunein (Hermopolis). History of the Patriarchs of the Coptic Church of Alexandria. Translated by B. T. A. Evetts, Paris, Firmin-Didot, 1947.

Following the example of Anianus, many of the inhabitants of that part of the city where he lived were also baptised. This roused the enmity of the pagans, and they wanted to kill Apostle Mark. Having learned of this, the Apostle ordained Anianus a bishop, along with three priests and seven deacons. He then went to the five western cities (Pentapolis), and remained there for two years preaching, where he ordained more bishops, priests, and deacons.

Finally, he returned to Alexandria, where he found the believers had increased in number, and built a church for them in the place known as Baukalis, east of Alexandria on the seashore.[18]

The Apostle's Martyrdom

It came to pass when the Apostle was celebrating the liturgy of the Feast of the Resurrection in the year AD 68 that the day coincided with the great pagan celebration for the feast of the god Serapis (the Serapion-Abbis Greek Egyptian god). A multitude of pagans assembled, attacked the church at Baukalis, and forced their way in. They seized Apostle Mark, bound him with a thick rope, and dragged him through the streets. They continued dragging him with severe cruelty. His flesh was torn and scattered everywhere, and the ground of the city was covered with his blood. They cast him that night into a dark prison.

In the prison, Apostle Mark was granted a vision of the Lord Jesus Christ, who strengthened him in his sufferings. On the following day, the pagans took Apostle Mark from the prison. They tied his neck with a thick rope and did the same as the day before, dragging him over the rocks and stones. Along the way, the Apostle

---

18 *Lives of Saints and Martyrs in the Coptic Orthodox Church: Saint Mark the Apostle* (n.d.). St-Takla.org. https://st-takla.org/Saints/Coptic-Orthodox-Saints-Biography/Coptic-Saints-Story_1648.html. Accessed 8 May 2025.

delivered his soul into the hands of God and received the crown of martyrdom.

The pagans wanted to burn the Apostle's body, but when they lit the fire, everything grew dark, thunder crashed, and there was an earthquake. The pagans fled in terror, while the Christians took the body of the Apostle and laid his coffin in a secret place in this church in Baukalis.[19]

In AD 828, the body of Apostle Mark was stolen by Italian sailors and was taken from Alexandria to Venice, Italy. However, the head remained in Alexandria. The Italians considered Apostle Mark to be their Evangelist and their patron saint. In Venice, the body was joyfully welcomed, and many miracles happened because of the body. It remained in Venice until a portion of his relics was returned to Egypt during the patriarchate of Cyril VI in AD 1968.[20]

Return of the Relics of the Apostle in 1968

In the tenth year of the patriarchate of Cyril VI, Patriarch of Alexandria, the relics of Mark the Apostle, the Evangelist of the Egyptian land and the first Patriarch of Alexandria, were returned to Egypt. After eleven centuries outside Egypt, Apostle Mark's body returned to the same country where he was martyred, and where his head is preserved to this day in the city of Alexandria, Egypt.

An Old Tradition at the Ordination of a New Patriarch

There used to be an old mystical tradition in Egypt, where, after being ordained, the new patriarch would go to where Apostle Mark's head had been placed. The cloth that covered the head

19 *Lives of Saints and Martyrs in the Coptic Orthodox Church: Saint Mark the Apostle* (n.d.). St-Takla.org. https://st-takla.org/Saints/Coptic-Orthodox-Saints-Biography/Coptic-Saints-Story_1648.html. Accessed 8 May 2025.

20 *Theft* (n.d.). http://www.basilicasanmarco.it/storia-e-societa/san-marco-evangelista/il-trafugamento/?lang=en. Accessed 8 May 2025.

would be changed at that time, and the patriarch would embrace the head and kiss it.

The significance of this tradition was that the newly ordained patriarch would receive a mystical grace from the head of the Apostle Mark because this head had once received the anointing of preaching the gospel from the Holy Spirit. The purpose of this act was that this grace would extend to the head of the newly ordained patriarch, allowing him to receive the same inspiration and anointing for his ministry and leadership of the Church as Apostle Mark, who was sent forth to Egypt to bring the gospel of salvation, had received.

However, after the body of the Apostle was stolen and out of fear that the head would be stolen as well, the Apostle's head was placed unidentified with other skulls of saints. With this, this tradition ended.

To Sum Up

The ministry of Apostle Mark and his spiritual activities were empowered by the Holy Spirit and revealed the diversity of his talents and gifts. Among his accomplishments and activities during this period were the following:

- He composed a liturgy for the Christians of Alexandria.[21]
- He founded the Alexandria School of Theology, which he started in the house of Anianus.
- He wrote Christian educational books, as well as the catechism books, and handed them down to the newly established church in Egypt.

---

21 This liturgy is sometimes used in Sunday services nowadays in the Coptic Church. It was later named after Saint Cyril, the 24th Patriarch of the Coptic Church in Egypt.

- It is said that he had entered Alexandria with his Gospel, which was written in Greek. It is the first and oldest Gospel, written around the years AD 40–45.
- He then returned to Jerusalem and met Apostle Paul during his first imprisonment in Rome and remained with him until the year AD 60 (refer to Colossians 4:10 and Philemon 24).
- After that, he went to Italy and preached the gospel in Venice. Because of this, the people of Venice love Apostle Mark and consider him the Apostle who handed down the faith to them. They also built a statue for him in the main square in Venice, St. Mark's Square. Later, they plotted to steal his body, as we mentioned earlier.
- After that, he returned to the five cities (Pentapolis) to follow up with and disciple the believers there.
- Then, he went to Alexandria for a second visit around the year AD 61 and remained there until he was martyred in the year AD 68.
- During this period, he also preached the gospel in the Oasis, Old Cairo (Babylon), where faith grew and spread widely, and new churches were established.
- Finally, he received the crown of martyrdom.

4. CHARACTERISTICS OF THE GOSPEL OF MARK

- It was written around AD 40–45, most likely in Galilee.
- It was the first Gospel written. Matthew took from it for his Gospel. Nine-tenths of the Gospel of Mark is found in the Gospel of Matthew. Luke also took from it for his Gospel. Half of the Gospel of Mark is found in the Gospel of Luke.
- The word *gospel* was used by Apostle Mark in an outstanding way that gave it a certain significance and meaning. The word was first used by Apostle Mark, then the other Evangelists and authors of the New Testament used it. The word *gospel* occurs in Mark 1:1; 1:14, 15; 8:35; 10:29; 13:10; 14:9; 16:15.
- Apostle Mark repeatedly used the word *immediately.* It appears in his Gospel about 40 times. This is because he wrote his Gospel mainly to the Romans, who were dynamic people and who held time as an essential factor. He succeeded in writing a concise and condensed Gospel, consisting of 16 chapters, which suited his readers at that time, the Romans. It conveyed to them the sequence of events precisely and consecutively in a way that would attract the readers to continue reading until reaching the desired aim. The aim was to believe in Jesus, the Son of God, as Mark proclaimed at the beginning of his Gospel (Mark 1:1).
- The Gospel is characterised by recording the events accurately and in a chronological and systematic sequence. The Apostle presented the story of Jesus, His life, sayings, and deeds, in an accurate chronological order. He used wonderful imagery. He focused on Christ's deeds more than His sayings. He mentioned only four parables that Jesus said, whereas he mentioned about 18 miracles and one long discourse about the end times (chapter 13). One truly marvels at this wondrous

personality that the Holy Spirit prepared with such great wisdom. He combined the skills of a historian with those of an artist—a combination that is not easily found in one person. The main concern of a historian is with events and their historical sequence, whereas the nature of an artist is spontaneous and contemplative, preoccupied with images and scenes. This personality of an artist is quite contrary to that of a historian; hence, it is difficult to be combined in one person except through the work of the Holy Spirit. In addition to this, Apostle Mark had insight and the ability to outline his aims clearly.

- Apostle Mark's main aim in writing his Gospel was to proclaim Christ as the Messiah, the Son of God, who is strengthened with power from above. Thus, he began his Gospel by saying: *'The beginning of the Gospel of Jesus Christ, the Son of God'* (Mark 1:1).

He referred to this aim again throughout the course of his Gospel in order to keep it alive and vivid throughout.

These words echo the words that Apostle Peter said in the Book of Acts:

> *Then Peter opened his mouth and said: "In truth I perceive that God shows no partiality. But in every nation whoever fears Him and works righteousness is accepted by Him. The word which God sent to the children of Israel, preaching peace through Jesus Christ—He is Lord of all—that word you know, which was proclaimed throughout all Judea, and began from Galilee after the baptism which John preached:* ***how God anointed Jesus of Nazareth with the Holy Spirit and with power, who went about doing good and healing all who were oppressed by the devil, for God was with Him****. And we are witnesses of all things which He did both in the land of the Jews and in Jerusalem,*

whom they killed by hanging on a tree. Him God raised up on the third day, and showed Him openly, not to all the people, but to witnesses chosen before by God, even to us who ate and drank with Him after He arose from the dead. And He commanded us to preach to the people, and to testify that it is He who was ordained by God to be Judge of the living and the dead. To Him all the prophets witness that, through His name, whoever believes in Him will receive remission of sins" (Acts 10:34–43).

Most likely, Apostle Mark heard these words from Apostle Peter because he was close to him during parts of his ministry. Mark knew his evangelistic aims, as we saw in his ministry in Egypt and other countries. He also knew the suitable plan for God's work.

- Due to his tender nature,[22] artistic imagination, historian skills, and high adaptability to different nationalities,[23] the wording of his Gospel was suitable in terms of its focus, its defined aims, its repeated use of the word *gospel* (8:35, 10:29), and its sufficient and detailed narration of the story of Christ's Passion and conveyance of the completion of the act of redemption.
- As for the general framework or outline of his Gospel, the other Evangelists[24] followed in his footsteps because his Gospel was the first written and known Gospel.

The general framework adopted in the Synoptic Gospels was to present the teaching of the Lord and the events that took place from the angle or perspective that served the purpose of writing for each Apostle. Apostle Mark followed the chronological sequence, whereas Apostles Matthew and Luke overlooked chronological order to focus on the main aim of their Gospels. Thus, they

22 John means *God is compassionate.*
23 Exemplified on the Day of Pentecost and during his journeys to different countries.
24 This refers to the writers of the Synoptic Gospels.

focused on gathering events and teachings that were connected in order to highlight the part of the picture they aimed to present of Christ.[25]

This was followed by an account of the Passion of Christ since the ultimate aim of the incarnation is the redemption of humanity.

This framework is followed in each of the three Gospels.

Apostle Mark's Gospel is unique in its presentation of the Passion of Christ. He recorded this account in 6 chapters (chapters 11–16), which constitute around one-third to half of his Gospel. This means that almost half of the Gospel focuses on the events and teachings of Jesus and the other half on the Passion of Christ and the story of redemption. Thus, it has been said that the Gospel of Mark is *the Gospel of the suffering Christ.* It has also been called *the Gospel of the martyrs,* as it was often given to martyrs who were imprisoned and kept in custody, so that they would read it and be comforted and strengthened by it before facing their death sentence.

The Gospel of Mark mentions around 16–18 miracles. This number is approximate because scholars hold different views on whether to consider some stories as miracles or as events related to the Lord Himself, such as Peter walking on the water and the transfiguration.

There are two miracles, which are mentioned only in the Gospel of Mark, but not mentioned in the other Gospels:

- The healing of the deaf and mute man (7:31–37)
- The healing of the blind man at Bethsaida (8:22–26)

25 Refer to what was mentioned earlier about the cherubim and the symbols of the Gospels.

There is also a parable mentioned only in the Gospel of Mark but not in the other Gospels, which is the parable of the growing seed (4:26–29).

Final Note

It is said that Apostle Mark copied from the writings of Apostle Peter. However, this was the view only of a bishop in Asia Minor called Bishop Papias,[26] and, according to most scholars, was adopted by other people after him. Yet, it would be quite natural for the Apostle to have derived some events or stories from Apostle Peter, as the two Apostles were close to each other. For example, in mentioning Peter's denial, Apostle Mark is the only Evangelist who mentions accurate details such as *the rooster crowing twice.*

Apostle Mark not only took and derived from Apostle Peter in writing his Gospel, but he also gave to Apostle Paul, who was keen on knowing all the events related to Christ from eyewitnesses. Apostle Mark was one of those eyewitnesses. In his Epistles, Apostle Paul says:

> *For I delivered to you first of all* ***that which I also received****: that Christ died for our sins according to the Scriptures, and that He was buried, and that He rose again the third day according to the Scriptures* (1 Corinthians 15:3, 4).

26 Bishop of Hierapolis and a Greek Apostolic Father (c. AD 60–130)

5. CHRIST IN THE GOSPEL OF MARK

In this Gospel, we notice the following features related to the Person of Christ:

The opening phrase of the Gospel is remarkable, and it indicates the precise facet of Christ that the Apostle aimed to proclaim in his Gospel: *'The beginning of the Gospel of Jesus Christ, the Son of God'* (Mark 1:1).

We do not read this phrase in any other Gospel. This is a clear proclamation of the divinity of Christ. Throughout the Gospel, we notice the characteristics of power and miracles—Christ strengthened with power. Remember that the angelic power accompanying the Apostle had the face of a lion, one of the faces of the cherubim, the symbol of power.

After this opening verse, we read straightaway successive miracles from the very first chapter.

We read about:

- Evil spirits crying out by merely seeing Christ or hearing His words
- Sicknesses and diseases healed by a mere touch from Christ
- A leper being touched by Christ, who should not be touched because of the contagious nature of the disease, which is also considered a sign of being impure or unclean; by this, the leper is healed, cleansed, and his sins forgiven—a matter that is the specialty of God alone

A Comment

Christ performed many miracles whenever there was a need, yet He refused the repeated request of the Pharisees for a sign from heaven. This was because He performed the miracles as merciful acts towards human beings, whereas asking for a sign revealed the Pharisees' rejection of Him, their lack of faith, and their demand that He ought to prove His ministry. Such a request also serves the ego and opens the door for unfruitful disputes.

Thus, whoever wants to believe and open his heart without any prejudice or reservations will find in the deeds of Christ the proclamation that He is the Son of God and hence believe in Him.

In addition to this proclamation in Mark 1:1, we notice two other proclamations that Christ is the *Son of God,* which occur in the middle of the Gospel. One of the proclamations was said by Apostle Peter through the Father's revelation to him. He said: *'You are the Christ',* meaning *the Messiah* and *the Son of God* (8:29). The other proclamation occurs during the event of the transfiguration through the voice of the Father Himself, *'This is My beloved Son. Hear Him!'* (Mark 9:7).

In the opening of this Gospel, we also notice that the Apostle quotes Isaiah 40:3, *'The voice of one crying in the wilderness: "Prepare the way of the Lord"'* (Mark 1:3). This quotation bears specific significance. According to scholars, the second half of the Book of Isaiah (chapters 40–46) speaks about Christ, *the Messiah,* as the suffering Servant of the Lord. Thus, quoting this verse at the opening of his Gospel reveals that Apostle Mark wants to highlight that Christ, whom he is proclaiming in his Gospel, is *the suffering Servant of the Lord.*

We might wonder how Apostle Mark moves so quickly from the scene in verse 1, where he proclaims that Christ is the Son of God, to a different and seemingly contradictory scene in verse 3, where he proclaims that Christ is the suffering Servant of God. In fact, this reveals a mystery that is often unnoticed—the mystery of Christ emptying Himself. Christ emptied Himself and took the human form, yet, at the same time, He retained His divinity, meaning that humanity united with divinity as the God-Man.

Apostle Mark presents Christ as the Servant strengthened by divine power to proclaim the Kingdom of God. Being a servant is the human picture of self-emptying, and being strengthened by divine power is the divine essence of His divine Person.

To portray this image accurately and concisely, Apostle Mark reveals this purpose at the beginning of his Gospel by saying, *'Jesus Christ, the Son of God'* (Mark 1:1), then he moves quickly to reveal two verses later (1:3) the hidden purpose of the words he quoted from Isaiah, which is *the proclamation of the Servant of God,* who emptied Himself but who is strengthened by God's power.

Apostle Mark thus takes us gradually but rather quickly, through a quick, concise plot of short stories,[27] until he reaches the middle of the Gospel (chapters 8 and 9), where we find two successive proclamations of Christ's divinity: *He is the Christ* and *He is the Son of God* (8:29; 9:7).

The Apostle also uses the expression *Son of Man* quite often. This expression has a specific significance that is well-known to Bible scholars, which is emptying Himself: *Son of Man = Man + the divine presence.* The phrase *Son of Man* is taken from Daniel 7:13, 14. It is also a term that Jesus Himself quoted in His trial (Mark 14:62) because, for a Jew, this expression signifies *the divine presence.*

Thus, Apostle Mark presents Christ as the Servant who serves the purposes of the Kingdom of God in a state of self-emptying. Besides, he makes us hear the voice that testifies that Christ is the Son of God, hence signifying *the divine presence.* Thus, in chapter 8, he presents Him to us as the Son of Man = *God in a state of self-emptying.*

---

27 The Gospel of Mark is a concise Gospel.

Immediately after that, we find the account of Christ's Passion (chapter 11 onwards).

Mark mentions Christ speaking about His Passion in three successive places:

- Caesarea Philippi (8:27–31)
- Moving towards Galilee (9:30, 31)
- On His way up to Jerusalem (10:33, 34)

Then, he set apart the remaining part of his Gospel (chapters 11–16) for the events of Christ's Passion and the act of redemption, unlike the other Gospels, as highlighted earlier.

Hence, we see Christ as the suffering Servant in emptying Himself and in completing redemption. But since He is the Son of God, His redemption is complete and true because it is the divine redemption for humanity. In His discourses with His disciples, Christ *gradually* revealed to them this aim. As we reach chapter 10, in verse 45, we see that Christ proclaimed this about Himself, saying that He came: *'To give His life a ransom for many'*.

In the Gospel of Mark, we see the following:

- Christ did not reveal Himself.
- The demons revealed Him; for this He rebuked them.
- In the appointed time, He revealed Himself to the disciples before the cross.
- His deeds testified to Him.
- After the resurrection, His divinity was proclaimed together with His salvation—the ultimate aim.

The final comment about the Person of Christ is related to His divine authority as proclaimed in this Gospel:

- His authority in general, which is given to Him from heaven (11:27–33)
- His authority over demons (1:27, 32–34; 3:27; 5:1–13)
- His authority to heal sicknesses and diseases (2:12; 7:37)
- His authority to forgive sins (2:5–7)
- His authority over the law (10:2–9)
- He has the final word. The phrase, *Assuredly, I say to you,* meaning *Amen, I tell you,* was mentioned 13 times. He is *the Word,* and He is *the First and the Last* (10:29–31).
- His absolute authority over life: He is all power, He protects us, and He watches over us

6. OUTLINE OF THE GOSPEL OF MARK

▪ General Outline

A. The ministry in Galilee (chapters 1–9)

B. The ministry in Perea (chapter 10)

C. The ministry in Jerusalem (chapters 11–16)

▪ Detailed Outline

1. The Beginning of the Ministry (1:1–13)

- John the Baptist
- The baptism of Christ
- The temptation of Christ

2. Christ's Ministry in Galilee (1:14; 8:26)

- Places situated around the Sea of Galilee (1:14; 5:43)
- Places away from the Sea of Galilee (6:1; 8:26)

3. The Beginning of the Gospel of the Passion (8:27; 10:45)

- Revealing the Messiah (Peter's confession) and Christ mentioning His sufferings for the first time (8:27–33)
- Bringing awareness of the path of following Christ: It is a path of discipleship and bearing the cross (8:34–38)
- The transfiguration and the miracle of healing the boy with a mute spirit in the valley after descending from the mountain (9:1–29)
- Mentioning Christ's Passion for the second time (9:30–32)

- Important issues:
  - o Who is the greatest? (9:33–37)
  - o Divisions (9:38–41)
  - o Stumbling blocks (9:42–48)
  - o Godliness as salt (9:49–50)
- Ministry in Perea (10:1–31), which included some delicate issues:
  - o Divorce and adultery (10:1–12)
  - o The status of children in the Kingdom of God (10:13–16)
  - o Riches and the willingness to leave behind for the sake of Christ: the inheritance of eternal life (10:17–31)
- Ministry in Jerusalem: on the way up to Jerusalem, entering Jerusalem (10:32–52):
  - o Going up to Jerusalem—Christ mentioned His sufferings for the third time (10:32–34)
  - o The request of James and John and the reaction of the other ten disciples to it—again the issue of who is the greatest[28] (10:35–45)
  - o The actual entering into Jerusalem: healing Bartimaeus, the blind man in Jericho (10:46–52)

4. Discourses in Jerusalem (Chapters 11–13)

The Passion Week has already begun. The events include:

- Entering Jerusalem, cursing the fig tree, and cleansing the temple (11:1–26)
- Teaching in Jerusalem (11:27–12:44)

---

28 This is one of man's biggest problems. We encounter it both in spiritual and material matters.

This section includes five discussions or disputes:

- First dispute: members of the Jewish council questioned Jesus, *'By what authority are you doing these things?'*; the parable of the wicked vinedressers (11:27–12:12)
- Second dispute: the Pharisees and Herodians about whether to give taxes to Caesar or not (12:13–17)
- Third dispute: the Sadducees about the resurrection of the dead (12:18–27)
- Fourth dispute: one of the teachers of the law about the most important commandment (12:28–34)
- Fifth discussion, initiated by Christ about:
    - Whether the Christ is the son of David or the Lord of David (12:35–37)
    - The hypocrisy of the teachers of the law and the widow's two mites, as a discourse with His disciples (12:38–44)

There is also a long discourse about the end times (chapter 13).

5. The Story of the Crucifixion and Resurrection (Chapters 14–16)

In chapter 15, our attention is drawn to the comment made by the Gentile centurion to proclaim one more time that Christ is the Son of God: *'Truly this man was the Son of God!'* (15:39).

Passion Week in the Synoptic Gospels and the Gospel of Mark

- Jesus entering Jerusalem
- Jesus cursing the fig tree
- Jesus cleansing the temple

Since Apostle Mark wrote the events in chronological order, we notice some differences in his Gospel compared with the other Gospels, as we will see later.

Apostles Matthew and Luke, on the other hand, recorded the events according to the particular revelation about Christ that they wanted to proclaim and highlight. Thus, they arranged the events in a way that served this purpose. Apostle Luke, for example, mentioned *cursing the fig tree* in chapter 13 of his Gospel, hence placing this event separately, not with the events of the last week of Christ's Passion. This order served the purpose of his Gospel because he wanted to show Christ as a friend of humanity and an intercessor on behalf of humanity.

Apostle John mentioned *cleansing the temple* at the beginning of his Gospel (John 2). According to some scholars, Jesus cleansed the temple twice. The first time was at the beginning of His ministry, and the second was towards the end of His ministry. However, Apostle John was more concerned with mentioning the first occurrence because this suited the purpose of his Gospel and did not mention the second time.

According to the account of the Gospel of Mark, the sequence of the events of the Passion Week went as follows:

- **Entering Jerusalem (Palm Sunday)**

Jesus entered Jerusalem and looked around at everything. This was an examining and affectionate farewell look. According to Luke, He wept.[29] He then returned to Bethany.

---

29 Luke 19:41

• **Monday**

He cursed the fig tree on His way, then entered the temple and cleansed it.

• **Tuesday**

Jesus returned in the morning, passed by the fig tree, and saw that it had withered. The withering had happened immediately after He cursed it the day before, and this is what Apostle Matthew highlights in order to clarify the authority of the word of Jesus.[30] Apostle Mark, on the other hand, intended to show the chronological order, hence highlighting the time the disciples saw the withering of the tree the next day. In actual fact, the tree had withered immediately after they had turned their backs to it to continue their walk towards the temple the day before.

On Tuesday, when the disciples saw that the fig tree had withered, they spoke to the Master about it with astonishment. Thus, He spoke to them about faith. They then went to the temple and continued the discourses recorded in chapters 12 and 13.

• **Wednesday–Friday**

- Plotting to arrest Jesus
- The Lord's Supper and washing the disciples' feet
- The crucifixion: There is no difference in how the Gospels recorded this part.
- The resurrection early on Sunday

30 Matthew 21:19

Part IV

DETAILED REVELATORY STUDY OF THE GOSPEL OF MARK

The two main aims of studying Scripture are to know more about Christ our Saviour and to discover the way of salvation more and more. If we lose these two main aims, the study becomes either intellectual, allowing us to gain some knowledge in our minds, or contemplative, giving us the chance to perceive spiritual insights into some passages. There is indeed no harm in studies of these kinds. The intellectual study is necessary as it opens new horizons in understanding the Gospel, and the spiritual insights and meditations are also necessary because they stir our spirit. However, the main aim of each book of Scripture remains to be *to know Christ our Saviour* and *to discover the way of salvation*. Consequently, this helps us to walk steadfastly in the spiritual path and to abide in Christ as a Saviour and a way to salvation, for He is the Way, the Truth, and the Life.[31]

Based on this approach, we will begin the revelatory study of the Gospel of Mark.

Apostle Mark's eyes were fixed on particular aspects of Christ, and in this lies the richness of his Gospel. It actually conveys two main aspects about Christ:

1. The Ministry of Christ (Mark 1–10)
2. Christ's Redemption (Mark 11–16)

Therefore, we will follow this outline in our study.

---

31 John 14:6

1. THE MINISTRY OF CHRIST (MARK 1–10:31)

A. The Aim of Christ's Ministry (Mark 1:1–20)

▪ The Aim of Christ's Ministry is Revealed (Mark 1:1)

The aim of Christ's ministry is highlighted in the very first verse of the Gospel: *'Jesus Christ, the Son of God'* (Mark 1:1). Without knowing that *Jesus* is the *Son of God,* there is no salvation for us. The opening of the Gospel[32] is concise, but, at the same time, it is deep and full of meanings: *'The beginning of the gospel of Jesus Christ, the Son of God.'*

▪ A Promise for the Servants of the Lord and Preparing the Way for Ministry (Mark 1:2–8)

In these verses, Apostle Mark mentions a promise:

> *Behold, I send my messenger*[33] *before Your face, who will prepare Your way before You* (Mark 1:2).

The Apostle is speaking here about John the Baptist. Yet, this promise is also granted to every believer in Christ. According to the conviction of the Early Fathers of the Church, every person who is set apart to serve the gospel is assigned an angel to help him in his ministry. This angel is different from the angel assigned to each person at baptism.

Based on this promise in Mark 1:2, the Early Fathers of the Church understood that when a person is set apart to be a monk, a priest, or a servant of the gospel, he is given an angel to support his particular ministry. At the same time, we ourselves are considered

---

32 The other three Gospels begin differently.

33 In the original Greek, the word is *angel.*

angels or messengers, preparing for the second coming of Christ, as John the Baptist was a messenger preparing for Christ's first coming.

Now, we want to focus on the things we can learn from Apostle Mark's highlights regarding Christ's ministry.

When the Apostle speaks about Christ as a Servant, he does so to highlight to us that we ought to fix our eyes on Christ and walk in His path. If we want to minister according to God's plan, we should follow Christ's approach. However, we should not try to understand this approach intellectually but rather fix our eyes on Him and absorb the Spirit of Christ[34] in our inner being. Consequently, we will find our feet walking spontaneously according to His ways and His approach because the grace of ministering the gospel will come to our hearts and lead us in the footsteps of the Lord. Hence, our ministry of the gospel will become like the ministry of Christ on earth when He preached the Kingdom of God.

Prayer:

Lord, I desire that every time I minister the gospel, I will have a deep sense of reverence. Many a time have I ministered the gospel with a self-centered and senseless heart.

O Lord, I greatly need for my heart to become reverent each time I take my Bible and visit someone.

O Lord, this ministry is much bigger than me, for I desire it to be truly the preaching of the good news. I am much weaker than this, but I rely on the heavenly support given to me by Your angels[35] who

34 Romans 8:9b

35 According to Scripture (Exodus 23:20, 21), the angel bears God's presence and His name.

walk before me, and Your Holy Spirit who leads me. Walk before me, O Lord,[36] for this will open the hearts of people even before opening the doors of ministry and will give authority to my words that they may bear fruits of salvation.

▪ Jesus is Our Example (Mark 1:9–15)

We need to know how Christ walked so that we can follow in His footsteps.[37]

How did Christ walk?

We can sum it up in two words: *self-emptying* and *seclusion.*

The theological truth about Christ emptying Himself referred to in Philippians 2:7 is proclaimed in the Gospel of Mark as well. The path of Christ is that He *is the Servant of the Lord.* This is the core of the Gospel of Mark, and this is also how Isaiah portrayed the Messiah.

Christ also gave utmost importance to seclusion times. He began His ministry by going into the wilderness. Also, the Gospel of Mark mentions more than once that Jesus would rise up very early and go to the mountain to pray.[38]

Thus, we can see that the path of Christ is that of self-emptying and seclusion.

If we wish to live and minister like Christ, we need to search our inner response and attitude towards self-emptying, self-denial, and our desire for self-glory. We also need to examine ourselves regarding seclusion times and whether we are committed to taking regular seclusion times.

---

36 Isaiah 45:2

37 1 Peter 2:21

38 Mark 1:35

Jesus took many times of seclusion. It is written on one occasion that He spent the whole night alone praying.[39]

In addition to emptying Himself and taking times of seclusion, Christ completed the confrontations with Satan for the sake of the Kingdom of God in order to proclaim the good news.[40] On several occasions, both in the Old and the New Testaments, we see the Kingdom of God being proclaimed in two ways: *battling* and *building*. The main book of Scripture that speaks about this matter is the Book of Nehemiah, where we see God's people holding weapons with one hand and building with the other hand.[41]

Since the fall, the whole world has been lying under the sway of the wicked one,[42] and the wicked one has put his hand on it as a robber. The work of the servants of the Lord is to restore the world to the Lord so that, as the Scripture says, *'The kingdoms of this world* [may] *become the Kingdoms of our Lord and of His Christ'* (Revelation 11:15).

By doing so, they will be taking it from the robber and restoring it to the King, Jesus. They will begin the battle by saying to the wicked one, 'Get out of this house; leave this land!' This land can be the inner land of the soul or a field of ministry. After they take the land, the first thing they will notice is that the land is desolate. Therefore, they will need to build on it. They can only build on it if their spiritual eyes are open and hence can see the state of the land and what needs to be done. However, if they do not have spiritual insight and do not see the spiritual work that needs to be done on this land, they will serve and preach randomly, and

39 Luke 6:12, 13
40 This point will be elaborated on later.
41 Nehemiah 4:17
42 1 John 5:19

thus will not reap any fruit. Because of this, we sometimes exert much effort in ministry yet reap little harvest.

We can now say that Christ is our example in:

- Emptying Himself
- Taking seclusion times
- Completing the confrontations with Satan to proclaim the good news of the Kingdom of God

As mentioned earlier, the first thing that Christ did before beginning His ministry was to go into the wilderness. What did He do in the wilderness? He confronted the devil and then returned to evangelise.

He explained this principle to His disciples by saying, *'No one can enter a strong man's house and plunder his goods, unless he first binds the strong man. And then he will plunder his house'* (Mark 3:27).

The *strong man* is the devil.

However, there is One who is stronger than him—Christ:

> *But when a stronger than he comes upon him and overcomes him, he takes from him all his armour in which he trusted, and divides his spoils* (Luke 11:22).

Therefore, we must bind the strong one to take his possessions—the souls that he has taken captive.

Christ completed the work of binding the strong one in the wilderness. His confrontations with the devil in the wilderness do not only reflect the different types of Satan's warfare against the children of God and the way to overcome them by the Word of God, but they also reveal the secret behind a successful and fruitful ministry *through binding the strong one.*

To understand how this can happen practically, we need to perceive what Christ did in the wilderness.

He was in seclusion, where he was fasting and praying. These are the weapons by which the strong one can be bound. As we read in Luke 11:22, the stronger (Christ) takes away the armour of the strong one (the devil).

How does he take away his armour? He takes it away through the counter-armour.

Apostle Paul highlights this matter in saying: *'Put on the whole armour of God'* (Ephesians 6:11).

Therefore, we need to put on the full armour of God in order to be able to take away the armour of the devil. When we take away his armour, we will have bound him. Christ bound the strong one in the wilderness. Therefore, as soon as He returned from the wilderness, those who were bound were immediately set free as soon as they met Him.

Many a time, we have foolishly and blindly tried to free the bound souls while we ourselves were still bound by the strong one, the devil, in certain areas of our lives! The devil has thus laughed and looked upon us scornfully, saying: 'You do not know what you are doing. You can do nothing for this soul that you are ministering to! Untie yourself first!'

As a result of this situation, we often struggle in our ministry, bear no fruits, and feel frustrated.

If the servant of the Lord knows how to be set free in Christ, he will be able to bind the strong one. The strong one here does not refer to the devil that Christ has already bound, but it refers to the confrontations that a believer faces in the field of ministry assigned to him, in which he has the right to bind the strong one.

▪ Jesus Calls Disciples to Send Them Forth (Mark 1:16–20)

In this passage, we see Jesus calling His disciples.

To sum up, the first main point, which is the aim of Christ's ministry (Mark 1:1–20), comprises the following subpoints, which are all needed for one to be appropriately prepared for ministry:

- o The aim of Christ's ministry is revealed (Mark 1:1)
- o A promise for the servants of the Lord and preparing the way for ministry (Mark 1:2–8)
- o Jesus is our example (Mark 1:9–15)
- o Jesus calls disciples to send them forth (Mark 1:16–20)

B. Christ Faces the Opposition to the Kingdom of God in the People, Unveils the Ailment, and Provides the Remedy (Mark 1:21–4:34)

The wondrous mystery of the Gospel of Mark begins to unfold and be revealed here. This concise Gospel is full of rich and amazing mysteries, which we will discover in the pages to come.

▪ A General Revelation About the State of the People and Their Spiritual Leaders

- The devil has broken in among the rows of God's people (1:21–28)
- The presence of various diseases and sicknesses among the people, afflicting the body, the mind, and the spirit (1:29–34)
- The loss of the main spiritual purposes, namely, worship and evangelism, from the people and their spiritual leaders (1:35–39)

When Christ went to the wilderness, He was aware of this scene because He had seen it in the Spirit. Thus, after confronting the devil in the wilderness, He began His ministry by revealing the opposition to God's Kingdom, meaning revealing the state of God's people at that time.

Apostle Mark wanted to reveal this point to draw our attention to how Christ ministered so that we can minister and live like Christ. Thus, he highlights that Christ is the Messiah and that the first thing He did in His ministry was to visit His people because He was sent to correct the poor spiritual state they had reached.

The state of God's people and their spiritual leaders is wonderfully described by Apostle Mark in 1:16–39, where he highlights that God's people had been invaded by evil spirits, had been afflicted by diseases and sicknesses in the body, mind, and spirit, and had lost the main aims.

We learn about the main aims from the passage in Mark 1:35–38, where we read that Jesus went to a solitary place to pray, and when His disciples searched for Him and found Him, He said to them, *'Let us go into the next towns, that I may preach there also, because for this purpose I have come forth'* (1:38).

Therefore, the two main aims are worship and evangelism.

Unfortunately, these two aims had been lost from God's people and their spiritual leaders at that time. The first general report about God's people in this Gospel is that the evil spirits had invaded them, hence they had become afflicted with many sicknesses from head to toe, on all levels—physical, mental, and spiritual. Thus, we read about many insane people (mental), demon-possessed people (spiritual), and sick and diseased people (physical).

Since the evil spirits had invaded them, this means that they had become captive and had many sicknesses. It also indicates that they had lost their health, their psychological balance, their mission, and everything that God had given them to proclaim Him on earth.

Likewise, the spiritual leaders did not know the aim of their lives. They were unaware that they had been called to be servants of the Lord and evangelists who worshipped God to gain strength so that they might preach to the people and serve the Lord by the power of the Holy Spirit.

For this reason, Apostle Mark presents Jesus as the example, pointing out that Christ the Messiah is the correct example to follow and is the One who reveals the state of the people.

There is actually no true ministry without the power of worship, especially in the end times. No ministry will succeed and bear fruits without sufficient worship.

After discussing the general revelation of the people's state, we now move to the more specific revelation.

- **The Specific Revelation of the State of God's People**

- ***The estrangement of God's people from God's ways and how the devil takes advantage of it (Mark 1:40–2:12)***

    - Revealing the essence of leprosy (Mark 1:40–45)—the sin that corrupts man and the effects of the devil's dominion over man
    - Revealing the essence of paralysis (Mark 2:1–12)—a sense of guilt, a paralysed will, and the need for forgiveness. Healing includes forgiveness, restoration of power, and freedom.

In this part of his Gospel, the Apostle portrays the people's state of being estranged from God's ways and highlights how the devil has taken advantage of this.

As an artist and a historian, Apostle Mark draws quick images, each image conveying an aim wonderfully and artistically. At the same time, the Apostle moves quickly from one scene to the other without neglecting the historical and chronological order, unlike the other Gospels.

Let us now see how the Apostle presents this specific revelation of the state of the people.

He begins by portraying a general picture in which the people were gathered together as a big crowd and were all sick. Jesus then passed among them to heal them, then this scene ends. In the next scene, the Apostle shows us only one person present—a leper. Then, in the scene after, he shows us another person suffering from a different ailment—a paralytic man, and so on. It is clear that the Apostle is focusing his lens on specific individual cases for a purpose.

In the beginning, when the Apostle speaks generally about God's people being sick, certainly the lepers and the paralytics had been among the crowds. However, afterwards, the Apostle presents the revelation related to these particular cases through the Lord's lens. We need to understand why he does this. Several times in his Gospel, the Apostle mentions that Jesus *healed many who were sick with various diseases*. If Jesus healed many who were sick with various diseases, why is there a whole passage about leprosy in particular? What else does the Holy Spirit want to reveal to us through this? This is how we ought to read the Bible, moving from the general to the specific revelation.[43]

Now, let us understand the purpose behind highlighting these specific ailments.

---

43 This is similar to studying science and biology, for instance, where we use the microscope to look at the slide as a whole, then we focus the lens on a part of it to see the detail. Apostle Mark does the same, using the microscope of his Gospel to highlight specific matters.

o Revealing the essence of leprosy (Mark 1:40–45)

Apostle Mark wants to highlight that leprosy symbolises sin that corrupts man. He also wants to highlight the devil's dominion over man in this situation. Leprosy reflects that the devil has struck man from within and has imprinted a stain of corruption on his nature.

o Revealing the essence of paralysis (Mark 2:1–12)

Note that leprosy is different from paralysis and also different from other sicknesses, such as that of the man with the withered hand.

What is the mystery behind paralysis?

It reveals the need for forgiveness and for experiencing its effects and results.

We often find that deep within us, we cannot enjoy the experience of having received forgiveness. We may repent and confess our sins, yet we often continue to blame ourselves and continue to lack complete inner peace and freedom. This often happens because we lack the assurance that Christ has already forgiven us. This, in turn, indicates that our fellowship with the Holy Spirit is weak because the Holy Spirit is the Person (Hypostasis) of the Trinity who bears witness within us of Christ's forgiveness and of all His acts of salvation. Therefore, if we do not have true fellowship with the Holy Spirit, we may repent, yet the fruit of repentance will remain hindered or faint within us. The Early Fathers of the Church maintain that Christ cannot save you without you.[44]

---

44 Though salvation is offered freely and richly to us, we need to respond to God's work, receive it of our free will, and work in synergy with the Holy Spirit in order to receive the fullness of salvation that has been granted to us, allow it to perform its transforming work within us, and not hinder it from reaching us.

Also, it is important to learn the path to true, genuine, and complete repentance. This also can only be done through our fellowship with the Holy Spirit.

If one has a true fellowship with the Holy Spirit, he will sense the conviction of the Holy Spirit within him, respond to this conviction, and thus have a true spirit of repentance. Without this fellowship with the Holy Spirit, one cannot truly repent.

Repentance is not merely confessing one's mistakes and sins and asking for God's forgiveness, but true repentance means a true change of heart and direction; it is *metanoia,* according to the Greek language, meaning changing one's mind and direction.

If one understands this correct approach to repentance, he will be able to truly confront himself, and his repentance will be genuine and complete. Also, if he goes to his guide/mentor or spiritual father to share and seek help and advice to overcome his weaknesses/sins and learn true repentance, he will be able to share without feeling ashamed or embarrassed. This is because he knows that true repentance leads to being truly released from sin and the effect of Satan, being set free and restored, and lifting his head after being freed from the shame of sin. Nonetheless, based on the teaching and experience of the men of God and the Fathers of the Church who learned the true path of repentance and its manifold dimensions, this sense of shame can be healthy and fruitful as long as the person has this fellowship with the Holy Spirit. In this case, shame and embarrassment lead to healthy brokenness, which, in turn, leads to inner purification and release from bondage and sin.

Based on this understanding, the person can be open and transparent with his guide/mentor or spiritual father as he shares his sins and weaknesses and seeks advice. Consequently, one can truly experience God's forgiveness and be assured of it.

Nowadays, God's people have many recurring sins that they cannot overcome or be released from. Though they may confess these sins and repent many times, they still recur. This often happens because they do not know how to repent and confess correctly through the fellowship with the Holy Spirit and a true spirit of repentance, not only completing the outer form of confession and repentance.

Furthermore, the main reason for sinning again and again is that we have not come to hate sin enough. If we truly see the ugliness of sin and hate it, we will repent and never return to sinning again. But, why don't we hate sin? This is because there is corruption within us.

Christ's forgiveness is so precious! If this forgiveness that bears Christ's redemption enters deep within us, it will cleanse us because forgiveness is based on the work of the cross. When this forgiveness penetrates the human conscience and begins to release the conscience and the soul from the stain of sin and its dominion over them, the soul is restored, healed, released, and rejects sin and hates it from within. However, if this does not happen, one will remain paralysed and constrained, unable to pray, serve the Lord, or do anything; and hence, will wither.

This is the mystical meaning and significance of paralysis.

- *The proclamation of the Person of Christ as the Messiah (Mark 2:13–28)*

How is Christ revealed in chapter 2 of the Gospel of Mark?

- o He loves tax collectors and sinners—those rejected by society (2:13–17)
- o He gives new wine in new wineskins (2:18–22)
- o He is Lord of the Sabbath (2:23–28)

In this part, we notice that the Apostle does not move the lens of his Gospel to other scenes nor does he present another person with a sickness or a disease. Rather, he begins to do something different, which we need to pay attention to because in it lies one of the mysteries of the Gospel of Mark. He presents successive images followed by Christ's discourses. The images reflect Christ's deeds and miracles. The discourses reflect Christ's words and teachings. Each image and discourse has a purpose. There is also a purpose in the sequence that the Apostle has chosen and a connection between the images and discourses in this sequence; this is what we want to understand here.[45]

What is the connection between the images portrayed by the Apostle and Christ's discourses that follow each scene or image?

To understand this connection, we need to note that the Apostle first highlights the general revelation of the state of God's people, then the specific revelation, which includes the essence of leprosy and of paralysis, and then records Christ's discourses and the proclamation related to His Person and Messianic ministry. What is the purpose of this specific sequence, and how can we benefit from it?

In fact, when we read about the leper and the paralytic, we can respond to these biblical passages by saying: 'Lord, I am a leper; I am a paralytic. Have mercy upon me. Touch me as You touched the leper; lift me and make me rise as You did with the paralytic man.' This is good, and if we say it by faith, we will receive actual grace. However, we need more than that—we need to know our

45 Since the Gospel is written through the inspiration of the Holy Spirit, the purposes in the passages of the Gospel should be connected. May the Holy Spirit help us perceive Apostle Mark's purpose and the connections he had in mind as he wrote his Gospel. If one is ready to spend sufficient time with the Word of God, waiting upon the Lord without getting bored, many things will be revealed to him. Hence, he will discover mysteries and enter into the richness and depth of the Gospel.

Saviour, who was sent for our salvation. Therefore, Apostle Mark begins to focus his *inspired lens* on the Person of Christ Himself, mentioning three of Christ's discourses (calling Levi, the question about fasting, and the discussion about the Sabbath), from which we can perceive specific characteristics of Christ.

In the first discourse, calling Levi cannot be the only aim of this passage (2:13–17), because if it were so, the ideas and passages would not be connected. The aim is made clear in the last verse of the passage: *'I did not come to call the righteous, but sinners, to repentance'* (Mark 2:17). Immediately before that, we read: *'How is it that He eats and drinks with tax collectors and sinners?'* (2:16). In fact, the Apostle's lens that is focused on Christ shows us three main characteristics of Christ based on the three passages or the three discourses in 2:13–28:

1. Christ loves tax collectors and sinners

According to any Jewish person of the time,[46] loving tax collectors and sinners was considered a *revolutionary act* because, while Christ loved them, Jewish people believed that any respectable person ought to stay away from them.

Consequently, according to the Jews, if Christ was a respectable person, He ought to have stayed away from tax collectors. If He did otherwise, this would indicate that something was wrong with Him.

Therefore, they frequently asked questions such as: 'Why does He allow a sinful woman to touch Him (Luke 7)?' 'Why does He let tax collectors gather around Him (Luke 15)?' In other words, they wanted to say that such acts caused them to be suspicious about His ministry.

---

46 These discourses took place in the presence of the Jewish people and the Jewish teachers.

2. He gives new wine in new wineskins

The next discourse is Christ's reply to the Pharisees' question regarding fasting, in which He said that new wine must be put in new wineskins.

What is the significance of this discourse and this phrase?

In this discourse, Christ wanted to tell the Pharisees that there was nothing wrong with fasting.[47] He Himself taught His disciples that *'this kind* [referring to the evil spirits] *can come out by nothing but prayer and fasting'* (Mark 9:29). Also, the first thing that Christ Himself did before starting His ministry was fast. This shows that He values fasting. However, the real issue here is not about fasting at all, and this is what Jesus wants to highlight through this discourse.

He wants to tell the Pharisees:

You do not understand what I came for. The issue is not fasting, but I am actually putting new wine into a new wineskin. Yet, you always want the old. You say, 'The old is better' *(Luke 5:39). You tell Me not to change the system you are accustomed to. You ask Me why My disciples do not fast and do what you are accustomed to. My answer is: I am doing something new; I am putting* new wine *into* new wineskins.

What is the wine and the wineskin, then?

The wine is the gospel, comprising salvation and grace and flowing with life.

The wineskin is the new man (the new nature) that Christ came to create in us (Romans 6).

47 This passage is often misinterpreted.

What does this new nature or new man look like? It looks like a vessel[48]—a wineskin. Is this vessel empty? Unfortunately, we often leave it empty. Yet it should be filled with wine.

What is the way to receive this wine?

The Word of God is the way to receive this wine. It actualises the presence of Christ in us through the work of the Holy Spirit. According to the Early Fathers of the Church, *the Word* is the Eucharist we receive and the Gospel we read.

According to this measure, what is the state of our vessels? Do they contain wine, or are they empty? Does our reading of the Bible lead to receiving *wine*, or is it mere reading, a duty that we complete? How do we read it?

It is written that the Gospel *'is the power of God to salvation'* (Romans 1:16).

What is the condition of our wineskin? Is it an old wineskin, meaning that we live by the old man, or is it a new wineskin, meaning that we live by the new man?

As New Testament people, we have received the new humanity; it is within us. It should be gradually revealed and manifested in us, for we have taken off the old man and have put on the new.[49]

Wine should also be poured into us anew so that our words, our relationship with God, and our lives may become wine.

What does wine imply?

It implies joy and a holy, fulfilling relationship with God.

---

48 Refer to 2 Corinthians 4:7 and 2 Timothy 2:21, where Apostle Paul uses the word *vessel*.
49 Ephesians 4:22–24; Colossians 3:9, 10

3. Lord of the Sabbath

Again, this concept is revolutionary.

The Pharisees often accused Christ of breaking the Sabbath in the same way they accused Him of sitting with tax collectors and sinners. They wanted Him to give an account of all this. In other words, they wanted to tell Him: 'Why do You oppose us? Are there no other days but the Sabbath to perform miracles?'[50]

Christ often healed and performed miracles on the Sabbath. Why didn't He avoid the Sabbath to keep matters smooth with the Pharisees?

We often think in such a manner, wanting to get on with things smoothly and avoid opposition.

However, the Lord had a purpose in doing this. He is the Messiah who came to correct the wrong concepts. What were these wrong concepts?

Firstly, these people rejected tax collectors and sinners, whom the Heavenly Father loves.

Secondly, they were keen on fasting without knowing its purpose. Fasting helps one to take off the old man so that the new man may be manifested, but the Pharisees were unaware of this truth.

Thirdly, they had a problem understanding the true meaning of the Sabbath. They were concerned with the outer form only. However, Jesus came to tell them that He is the Lord of life. Therefore, if any rituals or liturgical practices end up putting life to death and become merely an external formality, they are to be rejected.

This matter is crucial because it highlights that liturgical practices are channels to help us come in contact with the Person of God

---

50 Luke 13:14

and His grace. The Holy Spirit inspired the Early Fathers of the Church to put these liturgical practices in place so that through them we may enter into greater and deeper measures in our relationship with God and His grace.

Therefore, Christ was actually telling them that they had forgotten the Lord of the Sabbath and instead were paying attention to the Sabbath itself. He is the Lord of the Sabbath, and the Sabbath is made for man. These things ought to serve man's salvation, not enslave him.

Jesus came to the heavy laden to give them rest (Matthew 11:28). Why, then, do we sometimes complain that spiritual disciplines and practices are a heavy burden that we cannot easily observe? Why can't we complete our spiritual rule with joy and work out our salvation?[51]

These spiritual practices exist for the sake of man and his salvation; they are not meant to enslave man. Does this mean that we can abandon these spiritual practices and disciplines in order to live in freedom?

If we do so, we will fall into a much more difficult slavery. Our struggle is against the desires of the soul that seek false freedom, which eventually leads us to be enslaved to the devil. Thus, spiritual disciplines are our safeguarding measure. Yet, we should always remember to use them as channels for grace and life.

To sum up this point, we can say that Apostle Mark focuses his lens on Jesus, revealing to us that Jesus loves tax collectors and sinners, puts new wine in new wineskins, and is Lord of the Sabbath. This means that everything that Jesus does leads us to get in touch with grace and the Lord of grace. This will, in turn, lead

---

51 Philippians 2:12

us to know Christ as the Saviour and know the way of Salvation more and more.

After this pause to discuss Christ's discourses through which the Apostle wanted to highlight certain points related to the Person of Christ and His Messianic ministry, we will now go back to continue our discussion about the specific revelation. The specific revelation is related to the estrangement of God's people from the path and how the devil took advantage of this.

- *Revealing the essence of the withered hand (Mark 3:1–12)*

Once again, the Apostle focuses his lens on certain scenes that complete the specific revelation.

In the beginning, he showed us the leper, then the paralytic man, and here he is portraying *the man with the withered hand* (Mark 3:1–12). This part of his Gospel speaks about healing the man with the withered hand and other healings that follow this one (Mark 3:1–6, 7–12).

What is the difference between the paralytic man and the man with the withered hand? Aren't they both different forms of paralysis?

Physicians would assert that the former is total paralysis, whereas the latter is partial paralysis. However, we want to focus on the spiritual significance.

The man with the withered hand represents paralysis in doing good deeds. It is written: *'To him who knows to do good and does not do it, to him it is sin'* (James 4:17). This means that, according to the Bible, neglecting to do positive things is considered a sin.

The word *sin* in the Greek origin does not mean *iniquity* or *transgression*. It actually refers to someone pointing towards a goal but misses the goal. Thus, *sin* means *missing the mark*.

What does this mean particularly?

It means that every believer has to fulfill God's will and build His Kingdom. If one fails to achieve this aim and gets busy or preoccupied with other things away from this goal, he is in a state of *sin*.

Lust, stealing, lying, and the like are called *iniquities* or *transgressions*. According to the Greek origin, a *transgression* is a premeditated sinful act, whereas *iniquity* happens unintentionally, meaning without intended rebellion.

Accordingly, the man with the withered hand signifies that *God's people have become unaware of God's purpose for their existence on earth*. The purpose is to serve God's Kingdom and proclaim God and His love to others. Therefore, the hands of God's people should be stretched out to serve others. In the Book of Acts, we read that Jesus *'went about doing good and healing all who were oppressed by the devil'* (Acts 10:38). If this picture disappears from God's people, this means that the inner spiritual hands are in a state of withering and paralysis in obeying God and doing good.

Now let us go back to the question about the difference between the paralytic man and the man with the withered hand.

The paralytic man needed forgiveness. Therefore, Jesus said to him, *'Your sins are forgiven'*. He was in a state of sin and complete paralysis; he had completely deviated to evil and corruption and was in a *passive state*. On the other hand, the man with the withered hand, though his hands were shriveled, was generally in good health and could walk; he wasn't completely paralysed. However, his problem was that he was not living out the divine purpose for his life. Therefore, one was living in sin, while the other was hindered from fulfilling God's purposes in his life.

Apostle Mark pauses again after the scene of the man with the withered hand to reflect on a discourse related to the disciples. We will shortly understand the purpose of this.

- *Reflection on a discourse related to calling the disciples for ministry (Mark 3:13–35)*

Who are the chosen disciples, and what are their characteristics?

The Lord seeks those who live for positive purposes to serve His Kingdom. Therefore, there is a need to call disciples for ministry.

Seeing man's paralysis caused agony and groaning for the Lord. Thus, His heart moved in harmony with the Father's will and timing to call the disciples to be labourers in the Kingdom and stretch out their hands to do good. Hence, Jesus began to call His disciples (Mark 3:13–35).

Apostle Mark presents the scene of calling the disciples in his wonderful style as a gifted artist. All the Gospels mention the event of choosing and calling the disciples, but Apostle Mark presents this scene in his unique manner and style of a swift sequence to highlight essential principles, as we will now see, through discussing the characteristics of Christ's disciples and Christ's approach to discipleship.

1. Being with the Lord

To be with the Lord signifies having a continuous fellowship with the Lord. The disciples spent about three and a half years with Christ to receive discipleship.

2. Being sent forth to preach and evangelise as the Lord Himself did

Being sent forth to preach signifies that they have a purpose. The purpose is to bear the mission and calling of apostleship.

After the Day of Pentecost, the disciples spread out to the whole world to preach and evangelise because they received the heart of apostleship and the spirit of evangelism. Similarly, if our hearts are set ablaze with the divine commissioning to preach and evangelise the gospel, our souls will no longer be precious to us, and we will no longer care about what happens to us.

The gospel must be alive and manifested in our lives in order to be a revealed gospel and not remain veiled (2 Corinthians 4:3). If the gospel remains closed in our rooms and veiled in our ministry, would this be the gospel of salvation? How can it be presented as a gospel of salvation if it has not saved the person proclaiming it?

O Lord, do not let my gospel be closed or veiled. May it always be open and proclaimed at any cost. O Lord, grant me strength and grace not to count my life dear to myself.[52]

When the mystery of the gospel enters the heart, it begins to gradually swallow up the false sense of security, the false tranquility, the fears, and all other false things. It produces a consuming fire that deals with the indifference of the heart, causing it to wake up. As a result, the person begins to shed tears, having compassion for God's creation that has gone astray. This, in turn, leads the person to despise his deadened lifestyle and seek a different picture for his life. At this point, the person becomes no longer worried about the cost of evangelism and following Christ. This is what actually happened with the disciples.

---

52 Acts 20:24

3. Facing inevitable confrontations and learning to be estranged from all people and cut off from all ties for the sake of God's Kingdom

The servant of the Lord faces two kinds of confrontations: confrontations from his relatives and confrontations from people in positions of authority. The servant of the Lord ought to learn to accept suffering, face these confrontations, and overcome them.

This point is illustrated in this part of the Gospel through the confrontations that Jesus faced. As soon as He called His disciples, His relatives immediately went out to lay hold of Him, saying He is out of His mind (Mark 3:21). This is the first confrontation.

Then, in the following verse, we read:

> *And the scribes who came down from Jerusalem said, "He has Beelzebub"* (Mark 3:22).

The scribes, who represented officials or people in authority, came down from Jerusalem with an accusation against Jesus. After examining Him, they finally concluded that He was driving out demons by the prince of demons and that all He was doing was the work of the demons.

Then, Jesus' mother and brothers arrived. Standing outside, they sent someone in to call Him (Mark 3:31–34).

This shows that the servant of God faces a dual confrontation. He faces confrontations from those who oppose and attack him, and at the same time, he faces opposition from those who go to him with gentleness and compassion, stirring in him the ties of the flesh and trying to persuade him to leave this path, saying in a tender voice, 'Darling, think of your future. Stay with us. Leave all these matters. Be wise. We love you, and we are worried about you.'

This refining and testing that the servant of God goes through purifies him and makes him turn all the more to God. St. Augustine said: *'I sat on top of the world when I came to fear nothing and desire nothing but You.'* This is the true freedom.

Unfortunately, the human soul is often enslaved to earthly ties such as seeking its glory, honour, status, and relatives. These ties make the gospel veiled and not manifested in one's life.

Let us, therefore, allow the work of the cross to go deep within us and cut these ties. Let us submit to the divine work, let go of our rebellion, and fix our eyes on the Lord. At times, we may experience pain, and at other times, shame. One time, it can be a lesson to learn, and another time, a grace to be received. Through this and that, our freedom and setting apart are being completed, and we will become ready and prepared to be sent forth, saying: *'Here am I! Send me'* (Isaiah 6:8).

4. The disciples need to learn to bind the strong one

Realising their need to bind the strong one means that they should not forget that there is a strong one who binds people; thus, they must bind him.

To sum up, the characteristics of Christ's disciples as highlighted in this part of the Gospel are:

- Being with the Lord: Living in continuous companionship with the Lord
- Being sent forth to preach: Bearing a missionary spirit—a missionary's heart and mind
- Facing inevitable confrontations with their relatives and with the officials
- Binding the strong one: This is the law for releasing the captives

- ○ Being estranged from everyone for the sake of God's Kingdom

- ***The parable of the sower as an approach to serving God's Kingdom (Mark 4:1–34)***

This parable helps us understand the human heart and understand the different responses of the people we serve.

So far, the preparation of the disciples for ministry had been on the personal level only. However, in order for them to learn the principle and approach to serving God's Kingdom, they needed to understand the parable of the sower and learn that ministry is a process of sowing and reaping.

It would be foolish to think that we can sow today and reap the harvest tomorrow. When we think this way and see that it does not happen, we put all the blame on people, claiming that the reason for having no fruit is the unresponsiveness of the people to the message of the gospel. This only reflects that we do not know the principle of spiritual sowing. A farmer does not sow his land by simply putting seeds in the ground and then leaving them without looking after them day after day. Similarly, we ought to look after our spiritual plants and the seeds we sow through tears, birth pangs, and spiritual diligence in prayer for the sake of the souls as someone tending the land of the soul. We ought to learn to be patient because we will indeed reap a harvest at the proper time if we do not give up, as Apostle Paul says in Galatians 6:9.

We also ought to realise that based on the type of the land, it will yield fruits, some thirtyfold, some sixty, and some a hundred. In all these cases, the Kingdom of God grows. A fiery servant of the Lord always wants his fruits to be a hundredfold and does not accept any less than that. However, he must be aware that this is essentially God's work, will, and wisdom. God always wants our harvest to be a hundredfold because of His blessing; He always blesses us and blesses our ministry. However, we are sometimes satisfied with only thirtyfold, and we stop at this measure of bearing fruit for God's Kingdom. This happens because of the type of land of our souls and the siege that surrounds it. It also happens due to the fluctuations of the soul in her walk with Christ. The more one perceives these hindrances and learns to stand firm before them, the more he is released and the more fruits he will bear, up to a hundredfold.

Note that the other parables mentioned in this chapter highlight the same points highlighted in the parable of the sower.

C. A Distinct Revelation: Revealing the Deadly Dominion of Satan (Mark 4:35–5:43)

Apostle Mark continues to reveal the state of God's people. In this part of the Gospel, his lens focuses on certain scenes. As mentioned earlier, there was first *a general revelation* followed by *a specific revelation*. Here, there is a third type of revelation, which we will call *a distinct revelation*.

Apostle Mark was in the company of a spiritually trained group of people—Jesus' disciples—who were different from the rest of the people in their understanding of the matters of God's Kingdom. Besides, they were with Jesus all the time, which meant that they continually listened to Him and learned from Him. Consequently, they were able to understand revelations not understood by the common people. Therefore, in this part of the Gospel, we come to a deeper measure of the revelation, and that is why we call it *a distinct revelation*.

What is this revelation about?

It is about the deadly dominion of Satan over people, for he *'was a murderer from the beginning'* (John 8:44). In other words, this revelation highlights the different pictures or manifestations of death among the people and Satan's plans as the prince of death. Satan is the one who brought death upon the human race. He caused Adam, the head of the human race, to fall. On the other hand, Christ, the Prince of Life, as we read in Acts 3:15, wants to stop Satan's plan of murder, as we will see as He deals with these manifestations of death and provides healing and life.

Let us follow the various scenes in this revelation as highlighted by the Apostle. The main scenes are:

- The exposing of the evil power that caused the windstorm in the sea (4:35–41)
- The demon-possessed man of the country of the Gadarenes—complete possession (5:1–20)
- The woman who had a flow of blood for twelve years—death through continuous bleeding (5:21–34)
- The daughter of Jairus—death even in the house of the synagogue ruler (5:35–43)

In the first scene, Jesus was crossing the sea when a great windstorm arose. When we read this passage, we understand that Jesus crossed the sea in order to accomplish only one task related to a demon-possessed man on the other side of the sea. However, he was a special kind of demon-possessed man, as we will shortly understand. All the Gospels mention, in a general way, that Jesus healed many demon-possessed people. Yet, this specific event/scene is mentioned in the Gospel of Mark to reveal specific mysteries.

Before discussing in more detail the mysteries related to releasing this demon-possessed man, let us continue to look at the sequence of events. After healing the demon-possessed man, Jesus returned straight away, as we said. As soon as He returned, He found Jairus, the synagogue ruler, waiting for Him. This event is also significant, as we will see.

Jairus was not any ordinary person; he was considered the spiritual ruler of this land at that time. In every area, there was a synagogue and each synagogue had a ruler. Jairus was the synagogue ruler in Capernaum. Hence, in the spiritual language, he was designated as *the spiritual ruler of this land.*

What was his problem? What did he want?

His daughter, who was 12 years old, was dying. According to Judaism, this is the official age for joining the Jewish synagogue.

Alongside this scene of Jairus and his dying daughter, Apostle Mark introduces the scene of *the woman subject to bleeding.* Both scenes are recorded as happening simultaneously and are overlapping. They are mentioned together, or rather within each other, in all three Synoptic Gospels. This woman came in the midst of the large crowd to touch Jesus. Apostle Mark mentions specifically that the woman had been subject to bleeding for 12 years.

At first, we see Jairus pleading with Jesus, asking Him to do him a favour because his daughter was dying. Then, when Jesus was about to go with him to his house, the woman came, and she held Jesus up for a little while. Since this scene was going to involve a long conversation, Jesus stopped the procession for a little while, during which Jairus must have been tense. He must have thought to himself:

'I told Him that my daughter is dying; five minutes could make all the difference between life and death. Is it necessary for Jesus to stop? Who is holding Him up?'

No one was in sight yet at this moment because the woman who had touched Jesus had not been revealed yet.

Jesus must have sensed what was going on in Jairus' mind and must have wanted to say to Jairus: 'Stay calm, Jairus; I will soon let you know what is holding Me up.'

Therefore, Jesus stopped and said, *'Who touched My clothes?'*

Of course, Jesus' eyes had seen the woman, and He had understood her need.

Seeing that the situation would be exposed, the woman decided to tell the whole truth. She said it shyly because of her illness and because of other reasons that will be highlighted shortly.

Then, Jairus looked at the woman and must have quietly said with great astonishment: 'Is that *you*?'

Jairus must have remembered this woman because, according to the Jewish tradition, anyone with a bleeding condition would be excommunicated or cut off from the synagogue. This person would be thrown out and would not be allowed to practice as a Jew in the synagogue. This is because bleeding, according to the Law of Moses, signified impurity.

Such decisions of excommunications had to be signed by the synagogue ruler, specifically the local one.

Therefore, what would usually happen when a woman reported a situation like this was that her case would be scheduled for an examination, and then the synagogue ruler would determine and sign the decision to excommunicate her and disallow her from attending the synagogue. This had certainly happened with this woman. This, in turn, means that Jairus knew this woman, and both he and the whole synagogue regarded her a sinner; for, according to them, if she were not a sinner, God would not have allowed this bleeding to afflict her. Thus, according to them, she was impure, unclean, and deserved to be cast out of the synagogue.

Notice the well-knit divine inspiration in these two overlapping stories, as this will help us understand the spiritual significance and revelation in this biblical passage.

In the very same year[53] of signing the decision to excommunicate this woman from the synagogue, joy and celebration were taking place in the house of the synagogue ruler because his wife had given birth to a baby girl. While the bleeding woman was weeping, joy and laughter were heard in Jairus' house.

Let us live out these two events and try to imagine and sense how they went.

The years passed by, one year after the other. Every year, these decisions of excommunication would be re-examined and renewed if necessary; therefore, the excommunication of this woman was annually renewed. Also, every year, the synagogue ruler would hold a birthday party for his daughter. After celebrating his daughter's birthday, he would go to the synagogue and be informed that this woman was still bleeding; thus, he would renew the decision of her excommunication.

This continued to happen for twelve years. In the twelfth year, Jairus' daughter was due to become a member of the synagogue. At the same time, this woman reappeared before Jairus after twelve years and was about to be the cause of his daughter's death because she was holding Jesus up on his way to Jairus' house to heal his daughter.

---

53 Note that the woman had a flow of blood for twelve years, and Jairus' daughter was twelve years old.

At this point, we can deduce from the story that Jesus seemed to be speaking to Jairus' heart, sending him a specific message, as though saying: 'You have put this woman to spiritual death by deciding to excommunicate her and throw her out of the synagogue, and now you are witnessing/experiencing what death does!'

In this biblical passage, there is an apparent confrontation with death and a distinct revelation. Satan continually tries to put the human race to death. Jairus put this woman to death by excommunicating her and depriving her of worshipping God in the synagogue, and now death has entered the house of Jairus himself.

Let us leave this scene for a moment to move with the lens of the Apostle to another scene, the scene *of the storm in the sea,* because there is a connection between all these scenes.

How did this story begin?

Jesus got in a boat to cross over to the other side. Then, the Bible mentions that a great windstorm arose, and the waves were beating into the boat. There was a rage and a storm in nature. Jesus dealt with this storm by saying: '*Peace, be still!*' Notice that Jesus did not pray for nature to be calm but rather said, '*Peace, be still!*'[54]

Is the sea a person that Jesus would tell it to be quiet? It certainly is not; therefore, this phrase indicates that there was an invisible being there that the Lord was speaking to. Jesus was, in fact, speaking to a power hidden in the sea and causing this rage.

Therefore, we can deduce that there was actually an evil power there; hence, the language used was that of confronting evil spirits. Jesus was actually addressing the devil, but the disciples were not able to see him. This evil power wanted to drown the boat so that it would not complete its journey and achieve its mission. The

54 Mark 4:39

natural explanation that anyone would think of in this respect is that this was the rage of the devil against Jesus and His ministry. This is correct, but we can still discover something deeper if we look through this specific lens that we have been looking through.

To understand this deeper dimension, we need to perceive the nature of this evil power that had been causing the storm. Let us look closely at the events of this story to understand this point.

The devil knew that he could not confront Jesus because he would surely be defeated. However, this time, the devil immediately realised the purpose of Jesus' visit. We mentioned earlier that Jesus crossed the sea and went to that village to heal the demon-possessed man, and then He returned without performing any other task there. Therefore, the purpose of Jesus' visit became apparent in the world of the spirit from the moment Jesus stepped into the boat, and the devil immediately realised it.

Realising the purpose of Jesus' trip, the devil, who had possessed the whole country of the Gadarenes, knew that the One whom he feared and who always defeated him was drawing near.

Note here that the devil had not only possessed this man but had possessed the entire country of the Gadarenes. The devil had actually made the whole country of the Gadarenes break the Jewish law and tend pigs because it was a profitable trade. According to Judaism, pigs are impure and unclean. Remember that on the other side of the lake, there was the issue of *bleeding* which is also considered by the Jews as impure and unclean.

This evil power, which had damaged and destroyed this country with impurity and finally possessed one of its inhabitants (the demon-possessed man) to manifest its authority and cause the man to lose his mind, came out to confront Jesus.

Notice also that this demon-possessed man was naked. We know that sin causes nakedness, but also impurity causes nakedness. From the Book of Exodus, for example, we understand that impurity caused the Israelites to become naked when they worshipped the calf (Exodus 32:25, KJV).

Thus, the evil spirits made the whole country of the Gadarenes impure and made this person, whom they possessed, naked. It was as though this person was the main base of their work; they destroyed his personality and his mind.

Therefore, we can say that this demon-possessed man was the evil or satanic ruler of this country of the Gadarenes, while on the other side of the sea was the spiritual ruler of the land, Jairus. How lamentable this scene is!

Apostle Mark puts all these scenes together to portray this picture which is full of revelations[55] and which truly proclaims the gospel of Jesus Christ, the Son of God! Anyone who sees this amazing picture and the connection between these successive scenes would indeed say that this must be the Son of God and wonder how Jesus accomplished this big mission in one day!

He took the disciples with Him on this mission to reveal to them these special and distinct lessons. He wanted to expose before them the prince of death who destroys and damages. Thus, He first took them in the boat and exposed the devil when He said: 'Be quiet, be still'. He exposed him because he had been hidden, and then silenced him.

Jesus then went with His disciples to the other side of the lake and showed them what the devil does and how he destroys people.

55 The Holy Spirit, whom we have received, grants us spiritual insight by which we ought to read the gospel and go deep into its meanings and revelations.

The devil had caused this man to lose his mind, and he had also damaged the whole country of the Gadarenes.

Jesus cast out the demon from this man. By doing so, He broke the power of the ruler of the land and also transformed this man into an evangelist. When the man asked Jesus to take him with Him, Jesus said to him: *'Go home to your friends, and tell them what great things the Lord has done for you, and how He has had compassion on you'* (Mark 5:19).

Jesus also cleansed the whole town from pigs—when they all died in the sea. By doing so, He was as if saying to His disciples that He had finished this task, and they were to then cross over back to the other side.

On the other side of the sea, there was impurity and death. Impurity was manifested in the woman with the flow of blood, and death was manifested in Jairus' daughter. Both appeared at the same time.

Notice also that the Gospel states that the condition of the woman with the flow of blood *grew worse.* This implies that she would have inevitably died because of the continuous bleeding. She had gone to many physicians for treatment, but the bleeding continued, and it was incurable. Therefore, there was apparent *physical death* due to the bleeding, and also *spiritual death* due to being excommunicated.

The two situations—this woman and the demon-possessed man, occur in two different locations opposite each other. However, there appears to be one evil power that had been dominating and possessing the whole region.

The devil is usually based in the wilderness and desolate places. He was, therefore, occupying the other side of the lake, making the wilderness and the desolate area his headquarters.[56] He was operating in this desolate place and extending his activities to the crowded areas where the Jewish people were living. He was warring against them, and especially against their spiritual ruler, the synagogue ruler (Jairus).

The synagogue ruler had been carrying out his duties of excommunication which had often put people to spiritual death, yet he had not been vigilant over fulfilling his other spiritual duties, including protecting his people from the activities of the devil.

Therefore, at a crucial moment, Jesus came to help Jairus understand that he had put this woman to death, and then death came to his own house. It is as if Jesus wanted to say to Jairus:

'As the spiritual ruler, you are supposed to drive away death and eradicate it from your area. As the synagogue ruler, you are supposed to visit the people. Have you visited the people on the other side of the lake?'

Jairus might have thought to himself:

'No, I haven't visited them because I know that there is no hope in them. They are sentenced to spiritual death; they are actually dead. I have blotted them out of my mind. They tend pigs; thus, I went to them, rebuked them, and ordered them to stop tending pigs. I then left them, saying to myself that there was no hope in them.'

To this, Jesus would reply:

'Well, Jairus, you have continued putting people to death while they are still alive; thus, death eventually manifested itself in you. As the spiritual ruler, you were supposed to proclaim life. You were supposed to cleanse this country and show the people the true Messianic work. Every spiritual ruler should be a missionary, a small Messiah. You should have cleansed this country and cleansed those in it by the

---

56 Mark 5:2, 3, 5

authority given to you for serving God—an authority given to all those who serve God, both in the Old and New Testaments. If you had done this, you would have helped and protected this woman with the flow of blood; you would have found a solution for her or maybe you could have prayed for her so that My healing would reach her, instead of leaving her not knowing how to be healed. Your daughter would have also been kept alive and you yourself would have become a true spiritual ruler serving the mystery of life, and hence death would not have dared to come near your home at all. Yet I did not come to condemn but rather to heal. Do you now believe?'

At this moment, some people came from the house of the synagogue ruler to tell him that his daughter had died. What a great shock this must have been for her father!

As a result, Jairus as though wanted to say to Jesus: *'Didn't I tell You to come with me quickly? You stood here wasting time with this woman in whom there is no hope!'*

Jesus wanted to tell Jairus that this woman was actually healed because she touched Jesus with faith. Through this faith and this touch, she received power from Jesus; whereas, at a crucial moment, the faith of Jairus failed, and he thought that everything was over because his daughter was dead.

Therefore, Jesus said to Jairus: *'Do not be afraid; only believe'.*[57] These words indicate that Jairus had lost his faith. As far as he was concerned, Jesus could heal his daughter, but it seems that he did not have faith that Jesus could raise her from the dead. The woman, on the other hand, did not doubt but rather said, 'I only need to touch Jesus'; therefore, she was healed.

Since the woman was healed, this meant that she would be restored to the synagogue, that is, restored to God. When someone

57 Mark 5:36

was cut off from the synagogue, it meant that he was cut off from all spiritual matters.

Jesus had compassion on this spiritual ruler, and He healed his daughter. By doing so, Jesus broke the power of death from the spiritual ruler because He had actually already defeated the prince of death found on the other side of the lake. Effectively, Jesus was not raising the daughter of the synagogue ruler from death but was actually raising the synagogue ruler himself from death because he had indeed died while being still alive.

Where was his faith, his spiritual authority, his role as the spiritual ruler, and his duty to keep God's people spiritually alive and walking in the spirit?

In fact, he himself was dead, and death had manifested itself in his daughter. It had also been manifested in his people—the woman with the flow of blood, the demon-possessed man, and the people of the country of the Gadarenes who had been tending pigs.

It seems that this spiritual ruler had forgotten that he would have to give account before God for all of this.

In these interrelated scenes, we see that Jesus restored everyone and restored the land to God's Kingdom. This is a picture of the true ministry of God's Kingdom. Jesus did all of these things in the presence of His disciples to teach them and train them.

After seeing these scenes and perceiving this revelation that unfolds in such an impressive way, who can doubt that Jesus is the Son of God? Who else can bring this harmony, confront death, and confront the prince of death apart from the Prince of Life Himself, who holds the entire life in His hands? Then, this must be truly the Son of God!

Practical application:

Every believer has a responsibility to be a channel for the Prince of Life and protect his land from death, even if this land consists only of his family or his small household. Death has different manifestations. It can be manifested as sin, impurity, losing spiritual power (bleeding), straying from the divine purposes, or losing the fervency in our fellowship with God—a form of death that we often complain of.

Another important dimension in this whole scene is *faith*.

The disciples had lost their faith; thus, when the waves were beating into the boat, they cried, saying, *'We are perishing'*.

How could this happen? Is it possible that the Lord would choose them one day and let them die the next day? This is impossible.

Similarly, the Lord has called us to work in His vineyard, but where is our faith? We sometimes become despondent and our faith fades away because we fail to receive God's calling to work in His Kingdom.

Lack of faith is a big problem, as it often hinders God from working in us and with us.

The disciples had lost their faith, and the spiritual ruler did not have any faith; whereas some poor, simple, and lowly people were the only ones who kept their faith. This was exemplified in the woman with the flow of blood who exercised her faith and hence received power, unlike the others.

D. The Mission of the Disciples (Mark 6)

Main Points

- Jesus sends forth His disciples and strengthens them with power. He gives them instructions and recommendations regarding freeing themselves from possessions and having absolute trust in Him. The purpose of sending the disciples is the growth and extension of God's Kingdom. The results are:

- Great fruits
- Great opposition from the closest people and the strongest people

- Feeding the five thousand: In this scene, we see a complete and inclusive picture of serving the Kingdom of God and its results
- Fleeing from vainglory
- Praying on a mountainside

Seeing both the general and specific condition of the people at that time, which reflected the absence of positive work in God's Kingdom, Jesus chose His disciples and prepared them to serve His Kingdom, do good, and heal all who were oppressed by the devil.

The disciples' ministry is similar to Jesus' ministry and His Messianic work, as written in Acts 10:38: *'healing all who are oppressed by the devil.'*

Therefore, when Jesus chose His disciples, He showed them the deadly oppressions of the devil, which were discussed in the previous point. He taught them and showed them all the previously mentioned scenes until they became ready to be sent forth. Though their preparation is outlined in only one chapter of the Gospel, this chapter is equivalent to the span of a year or more. This indicates that the preparation for ministry takes time. When the disciples were ready to be sent forth to serve the Kingdom of God so that it might grow and extend, Jesus sent them to several places in all Judea and the surrounding countries.

In the scene of the confrontation with the devil, discussed in the previous point, we notice that Jesus did not stop at the point of explaining and revealing to His disciples what they needed to understand about the spiritual ruler, death, and the diversity of Satan's deadly work, but He actually brought about the *transformation* before their eyes.

In fact, when Jesus took His disciples with Him and revealed this scene to them, showing them what Satan had done and correcting the whole scene before them, He was, at the same time, granting the disciples the grace and ability to accomplish this very work themselves in their own ministry. We see an example of this when the disciples came back telling Jesus that the evil spirits had submitted to them in His name.[58] It is also written that Jesus sent them and gave them authority and power over diseases and evil spirits,[59] meaning He gave them authority to heal and restore the damages caused to human beings by the evil spirits, such as diseases, sicknesses, bondages, and oppression.

Chapter 6 outlines this ministry of the disciples and highlights its results. The results are: *great fruits* and *great opposition.*

Because the disciples were anointed with power when Jesus sent them, they bore many fruits and cast out many demons: *'And they cast out many demons, and anointed with oil many who were sick, and healed them'* (Mark 6:13). Thus, the fruits were: *healing many* and *casting out many demons.*

Where was the opposition coming from? Was it coming only from Herod?

No, there was another source of opposition, apart from Herod. In the first verses of this chapter, we read that there was opposition

58 Luke 10:17
59 Mark 6:7

from Christ's hometown, Nazareth. Jesus was unable to do any miracles there because of their lack of faith. In Nazareth, the people were saying things such as, 'Isn't this the carpenter's son who grew up here? What is this wisdom by which He does miracles? He is an ordinary person; we know Him; He was born here and grew up here.' This is the opposition that comes from the closest people, one's own family.

As for the opposition from the strongest people, meaning those in authority (the kings and rulers), it is exemplified in Herod.

Then, another scene begins in verse 30 and continues until the end of the chapter. It is the scene of Jesus feeding the multitude. We want to understand the connection between this scene and the previous scene.

The scene opens with the disciples reporting to Jesus, after returning from their mission, of the manifold fruits of their ministry. Thus, Jesus told them, 'Let us go to a quiet place to talk together and rest for a while.' However, in this place of solitude, a great multitude came and gathered around Jesus. There were sick people among this multitude. Jesus, the Shepherd, had compassion on them, and He began to teach and heal them. When the disciples asked Jesus to send the multitude away, Jesus refused and asked His disciples to give the people something to eat. Jesus then performed the miracle of feeding the multitude; afterwards, He sent the multitude away. Then, Jesus told His disciples to go to Bethsaida ahead of Him and that He would join them later. He then went up to a mountainside to pray, and afterwards, He joined the disciples and crossed over with them to the other side, where He found more sick people and healed them.

What is the significance of the miracle of feeding the multitude in the sequence of the events and scenes that we are following here?

Ministry always comprises two aspects: an invisible aspect, which is the battle, and a visible aspect, which is building. We witnessed an illustration of the invisible aspect in the opposition that Jesus revealed to His disciples earlier. Now, in this part of the Gospel, Jesus wanted to teach His disciples the visible aspect of ministry. Thus, He took them to that solitary place to tell them that they were now at a new stage, as they had already understood, learned, and practically seen what Jesus did in the previous scene. Thus, He would now be teaching them further new lessons in ministry.[60]

This new lesson is related to *the full picture of serving God's Kingdom*. This picture comprises teaching, healing, and feeding. To teach them this lesson, Jesus took the disciples to a solitary place where the multitudes had gathered and Jesus taught, healed, and fed the people.

When the Kingdom of God is manifested, it comprises teaching, healing, and feeding:

- **Teaching:**

The Holy Spirit brings pure teaching to God's people at all stages of their spiritual growth.

- **Healing:**

Healing refers to the healing of the soul, even before the body, so that God's people may become wholesome and restored to God's will.

This healing extends to the mind, healing it from darkness, straying, fluctuations, and division. It also extends to the soul, healing

60 In the beginning, Jesus taught them the lesson of sowing and reaping as an approach that they ought to follow in ministry. This means that the servant of the Lord ought to learn to be patient like a farmer who sows the land and waits patiently to reap the harvest. This was the first lesson, but now, there was a new stage and a new lesson.

it from the division of the heart, its sicknesses, and its struggles with its own desires and needs. This divine healing fills the heart and one's whole being with complete and deep satisfaction. Thus, God's people become truly satisfied, self-controlled, and preoccupied with heavenly matters instead of earthly matters. As a result, they cease to have inner struggles and impurities as they are no longer rooted on earth but are lifted upwards, and their eyes are fixed on heaven because they are heavenly people, learning to know God more and await their hometown. Healing becomes manifested in them.

God is the source of our healing, satisfaction, and teaching. This represents the complete picture of serving the Kingdom of God.

[There is still another stage in the lessons of ministry, which we will see through another scene. Shortly, Apostle Mark will show us the last picture pertaining to the Kingdom of God.]

Here, we should not forget that Jesus afterwards left the multitude and went up a mountainside to pray. Why did Jesus do so?

As mentioned in the other Gospels, after Jesus performed the miracle of feeding the multitude, people began to say: 'He is like Moses; He is a prophet! Is He the Messiah? We want to make Him king to free us from the Romans.' The Gospel of John tells us that Jesus knew what was in their hearts: *'When Jesus perceived that they were about to come and take Him by force to make Him king, He departed again to the mountain by Himself alone'* (John 6:15).

This reveals that these miracles and great scenes in ministry are often followed by *the temptation of vainglory*. This requires that one learn to flee from people at that time. Therefore, seclusion and quiet times are important as they purify us, help us regain spiritual power, and help us understand the truths in the light of God's countenance.

Finally, let us remember the following highlights in relation to serving God's Kingdom:

- Reporting to and reviewing the work with Jesus. It is written that the disciples *gathered around Jesus and reported to Him all they had done and taught*[61]
- Fleeing from vainglory through prayer and times of seclusion
- Proclaiming Christ as the Son of God. It is written that people touched Him and recognised Him, and said, '*You are the Son of God.*' Refer to Mark 6:54–56; Matthew 14:33–36.

E. Hindrances of Proclaiming God's Kingdom (Mark 7–8:21)

Main Points

- Legalism and hypocrisy (7:1–23)
- The gospel is confined to a small circle due to the lack of faith (7:24–37)
- Evangelising the Gentiles[62] for the expansion of God's Kingdom and addressing their needs (portrayed through three miracles), which are related to:
  - The devil's dominion and oppression
  - The senses being closed
  - Inner hunger
- Two disputes (8:11–21)

We have followed the various stages and steps of training and teaching that Jesus had taken His disciples through up to this

61 Mark 6:30

62 The word *Gentiles* is used in the New Testament to refer to all people who are not Jews. Evangelising the Gentiles refers to ministering to the nations. In this study, we will use the terms *Gentiles* and *nations* interchangeably in this context.

point. In this part, we will see how He took them to another stage, teaching them important principles pertaining to God's Kingdom.

Since Jesus Himself had been training them, they were now better trained and more sensitive than before and could comprehend the scene that Jesus was about to reveal to them concerning the hindrances of ministry.

What are the hindrances of ministry and of proclaiming God's Kingdom?

There are two main hindrances. One comes from the *inner circle* and the other from the *outer circle.* Here, the inner circle refers to the disciples who serve God's Kingdom which should extend and not be hindered. It should be the circle of faith. The outer circle is that of the opponents, represented here in the Pharisees, the teachers of the law, and the Jews who were gradually drifting to legalism. Therefore, the two main hindrances of ministry or of proclaiming God's Kingdom are:

- Lack of faith or the limitation and confinement of faith in the inner circle of the disciples
- Legalism in the outer circle

This part of the Gospel is rich and deep; therefore, we want to understand the divine revelation in it and not lose any of its richness. In fact, the Gospel of Mark comprises the greatest principles of ministry because it mainly speaks about Christ the Servant, as highlighted in the introduction.

The lack of faith indicates a lack of vision (the visions of faith) because faith produces a vision (refer to Habakkuk 2:2, 3; Hebrews 11:1, 27). If faith diminishes, one loses the vision because the vision is based on the well of faith.

In other words, we await the vision by faith. If we examine ourselves, we will find that when our faith is alive, it reflects upon our waiting on the Lord. Conversely, if our faith fades away and is lacking, everything darkens, whether in our spiritual life or our waiting on the Lord; everything becomes constrained, the vision is dimmed, and we even feel that we ourselves have shrunk. However, as soon as one shakes off and refuses to be imprisoned in this negative spiritual state, his faith and vision of the Kingdom of God are restored, and he himself is restored to life.

In Hebrews 11:6, it is written: *'For he who comes to God must believe that He is.'* Also, in 2 Corinthians 5:7, it is written: *'For we walk by faith, not by sight.'* Therefore, we need to train ourselves to live by faith.

If the faith of the inner circle fades away, the circle withers and loses its vision. What is the vision that is required from the inner circle? It is the vision of God's Kingdom and its extension. This vision is hindered when faith weakens.

What is the cause behind the hindrances of the Kingdom?

Part of the cause is revealed in the miracle of healing the deaf and mute man (Mark 7:31–37), and another part is revealed in the miracle of feeding the four thousand (Mark 8:1–9).

We read about the miracle of feeding the multitude twice in the Gospel of Mark, in chapters 6 and 8. What is the difference between these two miracles, and why did Jesus repeat this miracle?

The miracle mentioned in chapter 6 was presented to the Jews, while the miracle in chapter 8 was presented to the Gentiles. Scholars maintain that in the first miracle, the disciples picked up the remaining broken pieces of bread and fish in twelve small baskets, whereas in the second miracle, the disciples picked up the remaining broken pieces in seven large baskets. The difference between the two types of baskets (large and small) is unclear in the English translation. However, the Greek uses two different words that refer to two different types of baskets. One refers to *small baskets* (in Greek *kophinos*)[63] that the Jews made and the other refers to *large baskets* (in Greek *spyris*)[64] that the Gentiles made. Therefore, when small baskets were found in the scene, the matter was related to the Jews, and when large baskets were found, the matter must have been related to the Gentiles. Besides, the number 12 for the Jews referred to the number of the tribes of Israel, while the number 7 was known in the Greek world at that time as the number that referred to completeness and was hence associated with all people—the nations or the non-Jews. God is the source of blessing and thus He makes everything complete. Therefore, the remaining baskets in this miracle were seven to refer to God's blessing that makes everything complete. Also, in the first miracle, there were five thousand men. The number 5 refers to the five senses, thus referring to the responsibility of the Jews who knew the Law of Moses. In the other miracle, there were four thousand. The number 4 represents the four sides of the world, hence referring to the whole world.

Now, we want to look, through the lens of Apostle Mark, at the sequence of the events and passages mentioned in this part to understand their spiritual significance and deep meaning.

Apostle Mark intentionally records the events in the following sequence:

---

63 A *kophinos* was a small, hand-woven wicker basket commonly carried by Jews to transport food. (See G2894 in Strong's Greek Lexicon.)

64 A *spyris* was a large hamper, woven of rope or rushes, and was big enough to carry a man—as demonstrated when Paul is lowered in one through the Damascus wall. It is mentioned in the feeding of the four thousand (Matthew 15:37; Mark 8:8) and in the account of Paul's escape from Damascus (Acts 9:25; 2 Corinthians 11:33). (See G4711 in Strong's Greek Lexicon.)

- The encounter with the Syro-Phoenician woman in the region of Tyre and Sidon
- The healing of the deaf and mute man
- The feeding of the four thousand

These three scenes represent the Lord's ministry to the Gentiles.

Apostle Mark begins this part with the scene of the issue of legalism (Mark 7:1–23) and then, it is as if he abruptly moves to the scene of ministering to the Gentiles (Mark 7:24–8:10). What is the connection between these two seemingly unrelated scenes that succeed one another?

In fact, this sequence highlights important divine revelations. Apostle Mark begins this chapter by revealing the state of the Jews at the time, having deviated to legalism and neglected their mission of proclaiming God to all the earth so that His Kingdom might extend. In the meantime, the Gentiles were hungry and eager for the bread of life, as highlighted through the Syro-Phoenician woman.

Though initially Jesus seemed to reject her request to cast the demon out of her daughter, she persisted in her request, saying to the Lord: *'Yes, Lord, yet even the little dogs under the table eat from the children's crumbs'* (Mark 7:28).

Apostle Mark then moves on to recount the scene of the deaf and mute man who was brought to Jesus to heal him. Being deaf and mute indicates that he had lost communication with the world around him. Since communication is mainly conducted through hearing and speaking, being in this situation implies that this person had been cut off from life, as though put to death while still physically alive. This deaf and mute man represents the loss of human attributes because it is said that *man is a speaking animal,* meaning he can communicate and be in touch with the world around him through hearing and speaking.

From this perspective, we can describe these three scenes as follows:

- According to the Jews, the Gentiles were considered dogs and impure. Therefore, in this first scene, Jesus drew close to the Gentiles and cast out the demon from the daughter of the Syro-Phoenician woman.
- In the second scene of the deaf and mute man, the Gentiles were seen as being cut off from life. Therefore, Jesus restored them to life and healed the man.
- In the third scene of feeding the multitude (Mark 8), the Gentiles were seen in a state of hunger. Jesus, desiring to fill and satisfy them, performed the miracle of feeding the four thousand.

If we put the scenes of both the Jews and the Gentiles together, the whole picture will become apparent, and we can describe it as follows:

The extension of God's Kingdom was hindered because the Jews, who had the Law of Moses and the commandments, and who had a vision of the Kingdom of God and were thus supposed to serve this Kingdom, had deviated to legalism and become concerned and preoccupied with strict rituals and external observances, such as the washing of pitchers and cups and eating with unwashed hands. They had strayed far away from the true message of the Kingdom of God, which was to bring God's message to the nations and extend God's Kingdom. As a result, the Kingdom of God had become paralysed and was not extending.

Therefore, there arose a need to call new disciples who could serve God's Kingdom and bring its message to the nations. Thus, Jesus called His disciples, trained them, and prepared them for ministry.

However, Christ's disciples had a problem of a different nature. They lacked faith (Mark 8:13–21). When they got into the boat with Jesus to cross to the other side, they remembered that they had not taken bread with them and did not have more than one loaf in the boat. When Jesus said to them, *'Take heed, beware of the leaven of the Pharisees and the leaven of Herod'* (Mark 8:15), they thought Jesus was speaking about the material bread. Jesus, thus, reproached them, saying:

> *Why do you reason because you have no bread? Do you not yet perceive nor understand? Is your heart still hardened? Having eyes, do you not see? And having ears, do you not hear? And do you not remember? When I broke the five loaves for the five thousand, how many baskets full of fragments did you take up?* (Mark 8:17–19).

In other words, it is as if Jesus was saying to them:

'Didn't I feed the four thousand and the five thousand? Can't I feed you as well? How then do you still not understand?'

In the same story in the Gospel of Matthew, we read that Jesus said to His disciples: *'O you of little faith, why do you reason among yourselves because you have brought no bread?'* (Matthew 16:8). Thus, we can deduce that the disciples' problem was a lack of faith.

Jesus is in agony because the extension of God's Kingdom is hindered. He is the Servant of God's Kingdom, the Messiah who is sent to serve God's Kingdom. The gospel—the good news—is the proclamation of God's Kingdom with power through the Servant (the Messiah) of the Kingdom, who emptied Himself and whom

God strengthens with power to serve the Kingdom. Therefore, Jesus told His disciples that God's Kingdom was not extending.

To whom should the Kingdom of God extend? It should extend to the nations because they also have a portion in God's Kingdom.

What allows the Kingdom of God to extend? The extension of the Kingdom requires faith and visions of faith.

Who is responsible for this extension of God's Kingdom? At that time, the Jews were the ones responsible for bringing the message of God's Kingdom to others. However, they were absorbed in "formalities", which led to paralysis, preventing them from moving towards the aim.

At the same time, the disciples had little faith and thought that they had nothing to do with the Gentiles/nations; they were not concerned with their case.

We witness similar attitudes towards ministry nowadays:

Some may think that ministering to the nations is none of their business and that they should first attend to their own spiritual needs. For others, the issue of bringing the gospel to the nations may have never crossed their minds. Meanwhile, some may strongly object, saying: 'We will bring trouble to ourselves if we preach to the nations; we haven't even finished ministering to and evangelising Christians.' All these attitudes hinder the extension of God's Kingdom.

To Sum Up

- Mark 7:1–23 highlights legalism, or we can rather call it *hypocrisy* that hinders God's Kingdom. This hindrance comes from the outer circle.

- Mark 7:24–8:10 reveals the divine purpose behind the extension of God's Kingdom. God desires His Kingdom to extend to the Gentiles/nations. Therefore, Apostle Mark's lens focuses on scenes related to the Gentiles/nations; these scenes occur successively (the Syro-Phoenician woman, the deaf and mute man, and feeding the four thousand).

Through this sequence of events, the Apostle intended to reveal the needs of the Gentiles.

As mentioned earlier, the Gospel of Mark is *the Gospel of ministry* for all generations and the principles of ministry highlighted in it are valid and relevant for all generations.

Therefore, we need to look at our generation and ask: What is the need of the nations at this time and in this particular place? We cannot use our minds to answer this question because if we do so, we will put ourselves on a blocked path. This often happens in ministry, leaving the servants of the Lord with the impression that the door of ministering to the nations is closed and can never be opened. Yet, the matter of fact is that they are not entering through the right door.

What is the need then, and how can we discover it?

The point that we need to bear in mind is that we should not rush into telling people right away to believe in Jesus. We ought first to ask God to reveal to us their needs and grant us the grace to help them.

What were the needs of the Gentiles/nations as revealed in this part of the Gospel of Mark?

They faced three main problems:

- The devil's oppression and dominion

- Their senses being closed or blocked; people being cut off from life, and life having lost its meaning
- Inner hunger and emptiness

If the Lord grants the Church a rich grace that bears the power to release the souls from the devil's oppression, this would be the first step that would immediately open the door for evangelism. This is because if the Church possesses the spiritual authority to free souls from the devil, deal with the blockage of the inner spiritual senses, restore man to his wholesome humanity, and lead man to a state of inner satisfaction through the wonders and miracles that reveal and proclaim the divinity of Christ, who then can fail to confess that Jesus is the Son of God?! Christ's divinity will be declared through wondrous and supernatural acts and all that the Church will need to do is to bring this revelation to the nations and remain silent. As a result of this revelation, the nations will say: 'This is truly God; there is no doubt.'

However, if we do it the other way around and begin by telling the nations that Jesus is God, they will definitely resist.

If we minister according to the biblical perspective, search for the door, wait for it, and seek it, the door will surely be opened before us, and God's Kingdom will grow and extend.

These three scenes are followed by two disputes.

Two disputes:

In Mark 8:11–21, we read about two successive disputes. The first dispute is with the Pharisees (Mark 8:11, 12), and the second is with the disciples (Mark 8:13–21).

The opening of this passage suggests that there is an actual dispute:

> *Then the Pharisees came out and* ***began to dispute with Him,*** *seeking from Him a sign from heaven, testing Him* (Mark 8:11).

The Pharisees sought a sign, but Jesus told them that no sign would be given except that of Jonah. The sign of Jonah refers to the cross (death and burial). By this, Jesus was as if telling them: 'You Pharisees represent legalism and the solution for this is the cross.'

In the second dispute with the disciples, Apostle Mark does not use the word *dispute,* but it is quite apparent that there is some sort of argument and debate related to the issue of bread. At the end of this argument, Jesus said to the disciples: *'How is it you do not understand?'* (Mark 8:21). In the Gospel of Matthew, we read that Jesus said to them: *'O you of little faith, why do you reason among yourselves because you have brought no bread?'* (Matthew 16:8).

In the introduction, we referred to Apostle Mark's style in portraying events. First, he recounts the miracles and then mentions the discourses and teaching. This is exactly what he does here. He mentions the miracles that Jesus performs in ministering to the Gentiles, then he concludes this part with two disputes. Through these two disputes, the Apostle unveils:

- The hypocrisy of the Jews, who sought a sign because they had no faith; all they had was legalism and hypocrisy.
- The disciples' faith, which was weak and fading away; hence, they lacked spiritual perception, light, and understanding.

As a result, God's Kingdom did not extend.

In this part of the Gospel, we see how the disciples walked with Jesus as the crowd followed Him, that He performed miracles, and how the disciples were astonished by what Jesus was doing.

They were surprised that Jesus was healing the daughter of the Syro-Phoenician woman. They wanted to tell Him, 'What is our business with such people, the Gentiles? This woman is a nuisance, why don't You get rid of her?'

Then, the deaf and mute man appeared in the scene. Again, it seems as if the disciples wanted to tell Jesus: 'Where are You taking us? Why did we come to this region in the first place? Why don't we stay in our own region, Judea (7:24)? What is our business with such people? We are not supposed to have any ministry here!' Because of this attitude, Jesus said to them: *'How is it you do not understand?'*

Here, Jesus was not only referring to their lack of understanding about the issue of the bread, but He wanted to say to them:

'I can see that since we began our journey outside of Judea, your mind has been closed, and you seem not to understand what I am doing. The Kingdom must extend, yet you are hindering it by your lack of faith, while the Pharisees hinder it by their hypocrisy and formalities.'

This actually happens in every generation, and even nowadays we face the same hindrances. We cannot say that this hypocrisy or being preoccupied with formalities is related only to the Pharisees; we also may sometimes find our hearts preoccupied with the outer form and behaving hypocritically. The soul sometimes tends to adhere to trivial, soulish matters. According to the Bible, this tendency and behaviour is considered hypocrisy and hinders the Kingdom of God. If one comes out of the sphere of the spirit and faith and gets preoccupied with petty and trivial matters, this is considered hypocrisy in the biblical language. Hypocrisy means that the person is *of two minds*. To such a person, the Lord says:

'Do you desire to live for Me, or for trivial matters? You are of two minds. One time, you want Me and are preoccupied with the matters of My Kingdom, while, at other times, you turn your back to Me. At times, you are wholehearted with Me, whereas at other times, you are indifferent and your heart is cold. In the language of the spirit, this is called hypocrisy.'

The other state is the lack of faith. When faith fades and becomes weak, the mind is darkened and closed.

The explanation above is a picture of the hindrances of God's Kingdom as portrayed in the Gospel of Mark (Mark 7:1–8:21).

F. Proclaiming the King, Proclaiming the Kingdom of God with Power, and the Results of This Proclamation (Mark 8:22–9:50)

- Proclaiming the King and its results (Mark 8:22–38)
  - The miracle of opening the eyes of the blind man of Bethsaida
  - The gradual opening of the spiritual eyes of faith to know the Son of God
  - The results
- Proclaiming the Kingdom of God with power and glory, and its results (Mark 9:1–5)
  - The transfiguration and the events that followed

The aim of the gospel, which is also the aim of all the servants of God in every generation, is the extension of God's Kingdom. Therefore, after speaking to His disciples about the extension of the Kingdom and its hindrances, Jesus spoke to them about proclaiming the King and then about proclaiming God's Kingdom.

The Kingdom means the reign of the King. The King is Jesus. The word *Kingdom* refers to His reign over the hearts and the land, meaning that inwardly He becomes a proclaimed King over the hearts and outwardly a proclaimed King over the land. This reflects the complete picture of God's Kingdom. It is an inner, spiritual, mystical Kingdom hidden in the hearts and, at the same time, an outer Kingdom proclaimed on earth so that others may see it and believe.

The inner Kingdom is related to the believers and their fellowship with God, whereas the outer Kingdom is related to non-believers so that they may believe and be saved. Therefore, the Scripture says, *'the Kingdom of God is within you'* (Luke 17:21). According to the original Greek, the phrase *within you* means that the Kingdom is *in you* and *among you. In you* refers to the Kingdom within, in the heart, and *among you* refers to the Kingdom on earth. This latter aspect of the Kingdom is the responsibility of the Church. When the Church neglects this responsibility, she becomes weak and is opposed.

The Church ought to bear witness and proclaim God's Kingdom, and hence become the *queen*. Isn't the Church Christ's bride? The Psalm says, *'At Your right hand stands the queen in gold from Ophir'* (Psalm 45:9b). This biblical description and image indicate that the Church is granted honour and power.

However, if the Church neglects her message, she becomes restricted and cast down, she acquires wrinkles, signifying old age and withering, and she becomes exposed to disgrace and opposition from those outside the Church. This unfortunate state occurs when the Kingship of the Lord is not proclaimed within her and when she has not proclaimed the King to the earth.

Therefore, proclaiming the King inwardly and outwardly is the responsibility of the Church and is not an optional matter; it is a matter of life and death. If the Church possesses life, she either proclaims it so that others may live or hides it and hence dies, and others die as well. Because we have received life, we ought to proclaim it. Apostle Paul reveals that the core of evangelism lies in the sense of being indebted:

> ***I am a debtor*** *both to Greeks and to barbarians, both to wise and to unwise. So, as much as is in me, I am ready to preach the gospel to you who are in Rome also. For I am not ashamed of the gospel of Christ, for it is the power of God to salvation for everyone who believes, for the Jew first and also for the Greek* (Romans 1:14–16).

We are debtors, as Apostle Paul says, for we have received life. Therefore, we either share this life with others and hence it increases and multiplies, or hide it and thus lose it. It is the *talent* of salvation that was granted to us; therefore, we should not bury it in the ground but rather trade with it (refer to Matthew 25:25, 39).

▪ Proclaiming the King (Mark 8:22–38)

The first scene we encounter in this part is the miracle of healing the blind man of Bethsaida. Apostle Mark is the only Evangelist who recounts this story in his Gospel; the other Evangelists do not recount this particular miracle. It is also the only miracle in which Jesus healed a blind man in a different way than how He normally did. At first glance, the method of healing that Jesus followed here might seem unacceptable and incomprehensible.

Most of the healing miracles that Jesus performed were related to either blindness or paralysis, as these were the two main problems that people faced most. In fact, these two issues reflect man's problem in his walk with God, meaning that man neither *sees* nor knows how *to walk* with God.

When reading of the miracles of healing the blind people in the Gospels, we notice that Jesus healed them either by His touch or by a word of His mouth. The only time Jesus healed a blind man in any other way was when He healed the blind man of Bethsaida. In this miracle, it may seem as though Jesus did not possess the power for immediate and spontaneous healing with a word or a touch. However, this was certainly not the case, but rather there was a mystical meaning intended by this manner of healing, which we will understand shortly.

In this miracle, Jesus touched the blind man's eyes and then asked him if he could see. The blind man replied that he could not see well, that he could only see people like trees, walking. Thus, Jesus touched him a second time, after which the blind man was able to see well:

> *Then He came to Bethsaida; and they brought a blind man to Him, and begged Him to touch him. So He took the blind man by the hand and led him out of the town. And when He had spit on his eyes and put His hands on him,* ***He asked him if he saw anything****. And he looked up and said, "I see men like trees, walking." Then He put His hands on his eyes again and made him look up. And he was restored and saw everyone clearly* (Mark 8:22–25).

When Jesus healed sick people, He often did not ask them afterwards if they had been healed; yet, with this blind man, Jesus asked him if he was able to see.

Why did Jesus perform this miracle differently and what was the message that He wanted to convey through this method of healing?

May the Lord grant us spiritual insight to perceive the connections in His Word so that we may enter deeper into the mystical meanings of His Word and the mystery of the Gospel may be made known to us.

Let us follow the sequence of events to perceive the connection and discover the mystical meaning through this connection.

After Jesus healed this blind man, He sent him to his house, and told him not to enter the village nor tell anyone in the village about what had happened. Then, Jesus went with His disciples to the towns of Caesarea Philippi. On the way, Jesus asked His disciples: *'Who do men say that I am?'* (8:27).

The disciples replied: *'John the Baptist; but some say, Elijah; and others, one of the prophets'* (8:28). This reply bears special significance.

Jeremiah and Elijah are examples of great prophets. Elijah was clothed with power, and Jeremiah was afflicted with sorrow and suffering. For the Jews, both prophets referred to the Messiah. Elijah was the prophet of fire, and Jeremiah was the prophet of tears and sorrow.

When people said that Jesus was one of the prophets, this implied that they saw Him as one among many other ordinary prophets; to them, He was an ordinary prophet, who had a gift and a message but did not have a unique and specific characteristic. Moses and Elijah, for example, are mentioned together in several biblical passages. Moses was the prophet of God's Law and Elijah was the prophet who restored Israel from the worship of Baal to the worship of the true God. Jeremiah was the prophet who lived during the exile, carried the burden of Jerusalem, and wept for it. Other prophets had a message that completed the messages of previous prophets or linked one era with another. [The prophetic calling is amazing indeed. One prophet may be a pillar or a sign, while another may be the link between two pillars; both roles are just as valuable and important.]

Therefore, when people said that Jesus was Elijah, the Baptist, or one of the prophets, this implied that Jesus was seen in an undefined way. His image was not clear before their eyes; they were perplexed. Notice here the connection between the miracle of healing the blind man and the discourse between Jesus and His disciples that immediately followed this miracle of healing. This response of the people about Jesus was similar to how the blind man saw after the first touch, when he said that he saw people like trees, walking, thus implying seeing an undefined or non-specific picture or image. Similarly, when people saw Jesus and said that He was probably Jeremiah, Elijah, or the Baptist, this meant that they could see the likeness, but the precision was lacking.

However, after the second touch, the blind man saw everything clearly; things began to be defined, precise, and specific.

The same thing happened in the scene where Jesus asked His disciples, *'Who do men say that I am?'*

'John the Baptist, Elijah, or one of the prophets': This response or vision was similar to seeing people like trees, walking.

Jesus then asked His disciples: *'But who do you say that I am?'* Peter responded: *'You are the Christ.'* [In Matthew 16:16, Peter's response was: *'You are the Christ, the Son of the Living God'*.] This response reflected a precise and defined vision. The eyes of the disciples had received the second touch. As for the people, their eyes had only received the first touch.

There are two touches. The first touch grants the general answer and the likeness, whereas the second touch leads to a specific answer and a defined, precise vision. The first touch leads people to say that Jesus is the Baptist, Elijah, or one of the prophets (a non-specific vision), while the second touch leads those who receive it to say that Jesus is the Son of God (a specific, revelatory vision).

This is the mystical dimension of this miracle. It is not merely a miracle that reveals God's mercy and proclaims God's Kingdom. God's Kingdom is always accompanied by miracles of mercy, love, and divine visitations; however, this particular miracle is mystical. Mystical miracles are related to the Person of Christ, His divinity, His salvation, or His message.

When Jesus performed this mystical miracle, it indicated that the time of revealing Himself and His Messianic message had come. Before this, Jesus had always hidden Himself and rebuked the demons when they revealed Him because His hour—meaning the time of revealing Himself—had not yet come, as we read in the Gospel of John.[65] However, towards the end of His ministry, Jesus began to reveal Himself. Thus, we see Him, for instance, enter Jerusalem in a royal procession. Also, when the high priest asked Jesus, *'Are You the Christ, the Son of the Blessed?'* Jesus said, *'I am. And you will see the Son of Man sitting at the right hand of the Power, and coming with the clouds of heaven'* (Mark 14:62). For the Jews, the phrase *the Son of Man ... coming with the clouds of heaven* was a quotation from Daniel 7:13 that meant that He is God. From this, we clearly see that Jesus intended to reveal Himself towards the end of His ministry on earth.

How did Jesus reveal Himself? He did it through this miracle of gradually restoring the sight of this blind man. Through this miracle, Jesus highlighted that seeing Him as He truly is, as the Son of God, is revealed in various stages because this revelation requires His divine touch to the spiritual sight. As a result, the spiritual insight will be opened gradually, and little by little, the person will begin to perceive Jesus as He truly is until this perception reaches its fullness—the fullness of revelation and perception of Christ as the true and living Son of God: *'He* [the blind man] *was restored and saw everyone clearly'*.[66]

---

65 John 2:4
66 Mark 8:25

If we apply this to our own relationship with God, each of us ought to ask ourselves if we truly know God or only know about Him through some words that we may have learned and memorised. If we only know Him through what we have learned in the Creed and what we have heard about Him, this is merely intellectual knowledge in the mind, not a knowledge of the heart!

Man's real problem is that God is absent from his heart and soul, hence man suffers deep inner emptiness. If the human soul is estranged from the true knowledge of Christ, she cannot discern the appropriate food for herself. Consequently, she will feed on lust and impurities, as she has not found the bread of life. In John 6, Jesus says: *'I am the bread of life.'*[67] These words mean that Jesus is the only one who satisfies and gives life.

If the human soul tastes the bread of life, her desire for uncleanness will fade away easily. However, if the soul has not yet tasted the bread of life, it will be difficult for her to resist temptations and lust. Though the soul knows quite well that she is seeking the straw, she says: 'This is the only thing available.'

This attitude is similar to that of the prodigal son who desired to eat the pods that the swine ate (Luke 15). He knew quite well that what he longed for was merely pods and was not in any way comparable to the rich food by which he was nourished all his life in his father's house. He was the son of a wealthy man, brought up in luxury and accustomed to rich food! However, when he journeyed to a far country, he was obliged to eat the pods. He became stuck, as he neither knew how to leave the pods without delay nor how to restore what he previously had. He continued in this state until he reached complete nakedness. At this point, he came to himself and decided to arise, return to his father, and

---

67 John 6:35, 48

say to him: *'I have sinned.'* When circumstances became tight, the prodigal son was driven by divine mercy, not by his feet, which were completely paralysed at that point.

When the human soul tastes the living bread, the whole matter is resolved and her struggles end.

Where can the soul find the bread of life?

It is found in the Bible and the Holy Communion. When one receives this bread of life and then presents it to others, meaning one presents the mysteries of the Bible, which are satisfying and reviving, many will be drawn to this food. Consequently, the pulse of life will flow to the soul, the body, and the whole being, filling it with life and light.

This is the mystical meaning of the story of the healing of the blind man of Bethsaida, its connection with the scene that followed at Caesarea Philippi, and the connection between the two questions that Jesus asked in each of these scenes:

> *And when He had spit on his eyes and put His hands on him,* ***He asked him if he saw anything*** *…* ***Who do men say that I am****?*

From the above passages, we have understood that Christ is revealed gradually and is not revealed through the knowledge of the mind but of the heart. Accordingly, we need to ask the Lord for His gradual divine touches so that we may know Him all the more. He is infinite and there are no limits to the renewed visions we can receive of Him. Let us ask the Lord to increase our longing for Him and open our insight.

The Lord is asking us the same question that He asked His disciples:

'Who am I for you? Do you only know about Me or do you know Me as a living Person and as the bread of life, having witnessed Me in situations engraved in your heart that no one can uproot or take away, neither by sword nor by taking away all your possessions?'

In Romans 8:35, the Apostle says:

> *Who shall separate us from the love of Christ? Shall tribulation, or distress, or persecution, or famine, or nakedness, or peril, or sword?*

When we see Jesus, all the matters listed in this verse become insignificant and of no value. The more we long to see Him and know Him, the more we get in touch with the mystery of His divine touches. As a result, He will be revealed to us anew in a new form that will fill all our needs and fill us with His glory: *'And the glory which You gave Me I have given them'* (John 17:22).

A final comment on chapter 8

Verses 31–38 of chapter 8 speak about the crucifixion. In the introduction, we highlighted that Apostle Mark refers to Christ's Passion three times in his Gospel. This passage marks the first mention of this topic in this Gospel.

Scholars maintain that the Gospel of Mark is the Gospel of Christ's Passion and hence the Apostle repeats this story despite it being recorded in the other Gospels. However, Apostle Mark had a different purpose from the other Evangelists in recording this topic.

The Apostle mentions the following words that Jesus said to His disciples three times in his Gospel:

> *He began to teach them that the Son of Man must suffer many things, and be rejected by the elders and chief priests and scribes, and be killed, and after three days rise again.*[68]

---

68 Mark 8:31

The repetition does not signify that Jesus was merely drawing His disciples' attention to this matter because, as clearly stated in the Gospel, the disciples did not understand despite the repetition.

What was the Lord's purpose then?

Jesus knew that the disciples could not understand despite the repetition, because there was a certain blockage in perceiving this matter. Therefore, the purpose of repeating these words is that they would be recorded in the Bible for all the generations to come. Each of the three mentions of Christ's Passion in this Gospel has a special key, mystery, and value. The first mention is associated with *proclaiming the King*. The second mention occurs after the transfiguration and is associated with *proclaiming the Kingdom of God*. The third mention occurs at the beginning of Christ's entrance into Jerusalem and is associated with *the events of the crucifixion*. We will discuss each mention and its association with the events surrounding it as we come to it in the course of this study.

The First Mention of Christ's Passion in the Gospel of Mark (8:31–38)

What did Christ want to highlight here?

After illustrating that He is revealed through the gradual opening of the spiritual sight and that is by seeking Him, longing for Him, and waiting for Him to open our insight and reveal Himself to us, the Lord asks us if we are ready for the cost. The revelation of the Son of God is precious; it is a special mystery, yet it has a cost. Are we ready for this cost?

What is the cost?

The cost is to bear the cross.

What does bearing the cross imply?

Bearing the cross includes different stages and levels.

The first stage is to deny oneself. For the Lord to be revealed to us, we must deny ourselves.

Jesus said it directly to His disciples: '*Whoever desires to come after Me, **let him deny himself,** and take up his cross, and follow Me'* (Mark 8:34).

Other stages will follow, but this is the first stage. Each stage has its own special grace to enable the person to go through it.

If you deny yourself, He will reveal Himself to you, but if you reveal yourself, He will be hidden. It is either 'I' or 'Christ'. In Galatians 2:20, Apostle Paul declares: '*It is no longer I who live, but Christ lives in me'*.

Therefore, if it is I who lives, Christ disappears, but if Christ lives, I have to be hidden by being in a state of self-denial.

▪ Proclaiming the Kingdom of God (Mark 9:1–50)

The main theme of chapter 9 is the proclamation of God's Kingdom with power. This theme is highlighted through the scene of the transfiguration (9:1–13).

After our spiritual insight is opened, Christ will first be revealed to us in various situations in our personal lives. He will be revealed in various forms as the Bridegroom, the tenderhearted Companion, the Spring of faith, and the living Person. This revelation performs a true inner transformation within us. As a result, we become ready and prepared to receive the revelations of transfiguration. These revelations are manifold. Christ begins to be transfigured in our hearts in a special and clear way through various situations.

Therefore, there are two stages of revelation after our spiritual insight is opened. The first stage is to see Him as a Person, as the Son of God, and the second stage is the transfiguration.

In the beginning, Peter did not see Jesus shining; he saw Him in an ordinary form. Yet, the Father revealed to Peter that Christ is His Son. However, later, on the Mount of Transfiguration, the disciples saw the same Jesus bright and shining and in great glory, and heard with their own ears the voice, saying, *'This is My beloved Son. Hear Him!'* (9:7). This highlights that the revelation on the Mount of Transfiguration was different from the previous revelation, which was seeing Him as the Son of God. We cannot reach the second stage unless we go through the first stage.

Therefore, at first, Jesus is gradually revealed to the heart through the opening of the insight and through the situations that God allows for this purpose, such as taking His disciples to Caesarea Philippi.

In this context, we notice that Jesus took the blind man outside the village (Mark 8:23). Why did Jesus take him outside the village, and what does this signify?

In fact, this signifies that this revelation requires seclusion. Seclusion does not only refer to taking some quiet times, but it essentially means that the heart is separated from earthly ties. When the heart goes outside the village and is separated from all that is in the village, the heart can see Jesus.

After seeing Him outside the village, which is the first stage of the revelation, one needs a further step to enter into the second stage of the revelation, which is the transfiguration. Transfiguration requires not only going outside the village, but also ascending the mountain.

Therefore, after experiencing going outside, away from the crowd and noise, and gradually seeing Him until we see Him as a true and living Person, the Lord invites us to ascend the mountain with Him. Ascending the mountain refers to a *deeper fellowship with Him.*

Seclusion, which is the *first step,* refers to *quietness,* while *the mountain,* which is the *second step,* refers to *more worship.* Therefore, the need is for quietness and deeper worship. In the quietness, the world comes out of my heart, and thus I see Jesus. When I see Him, I long for Him more, and hence I am driven upwards. From this point of ascent, if I pour myself out in worship, He is transfigured to me, and the voice of the Father accompanies this transfiguration.

What are the results of transfiguration?

The results of transfiguration are highlighted in 9:14–50.

The first story recounted immediately after Jesus and His disciples came down from the Mount of Transfiguration is the healing of the boy possessed by a mute spirit. What does this story signify?

This boy suffered from fits due to being possessed by an evil mute spirit. In fact, the boy himself was not mute, but the devil who possessed him was mute.

But was this evil spirit really mute?

In fact, this muteness reveals the cunningness of this evil spirit. At that time, the Jewish people were familiar with the gift of casting out demons. If one had this gift, he would rebuke the evil spirit, and, with the authority granted to him, he would make this evil spirit show itself. Therefore, if this evil spirit was mute, it meant that no one could force it to reveal its identity as it could not speak. It also refused to respond to anyone who called it. This meant that this evil spirit had cunningly hidden itself so that even the person who had the authority to cast it out and burn it with prayer would not succeed in casting it out because it was hidden and had covered itself.

An evil spirit does not come out willingly, on its own accord; it only comes out because of the spiritual authority that burns it and compels it to leave. However, the evil spirit that possessed this boy was cunning and had hidden itself completely to rest secure and unrevealed.

This scenario of this demon-possessed boy and his parents is unfortunately common and often happens in such a way. As a result, in such cases, when the person with the gift of casting out demons prays, he does not see the evil spirit; thus, he would tell the parents of the demon-possessed child that the child is fine and not demon-possessed. However, in reality, the child would indeed be demon-possessed, but the evil spirit would be lying hidden. Consequently, the parents would think that their son is ill and therefore begin a series of medical examinations, entering into the dilemma of possible diagnoses without reaching any definitive answer or explanation. Their confusion and pain then increase because there would seem to be no apparent demon and, at the same time, the physicians would be describing the child's ailments as epileptic fits for which there would be no complete treatment.

Because of this, the father of this boy said to Jesus, '*And often he* [the evil spirit] *has thrown him* [the boy] *both into the fire and into the water to destroy him. But if You can do anything, have compassion on us and help us*' (9:22). In other words, the father was as if saying that they had done all that could be done but had found no solution. Neither religious people nor physicians had been able to help them. Now, the father was exhausted and did not know what to do. Therefore, he asked Jesus to have compassion on them if there was anything that Jesus could do.

People often reach this state of being completely drained when the evil spirit hides itself. This is one of the techniques that the devil resorts to when he desires to intensify his destruction of the human soul. He ruins the soul and then covers the destruction so that no one can reach this soul. In this part of his Gospel, the Apostle reveals the solution for these situations, as we shall explain shortly.

At that time, Jesus had been performing various miracles in His ministry. Why did the Apostle leave out all the other miracles that Jesus performed after the event of transfiguration and focus his lens only on this demon-possessed boy? It is clear that the sequence in which the events are recorded is an important factor for the Apostle.

[Note that the Gospels of Matthew and Luke recount this story but not in the same depth of detail as the Gospel of Mark.]

In fact, the Apostle wanted to highlight an important point pertaining to ministry since this is the Gospel of the Kingdom ministry. As ministers of God's Kingdom, we need to learn from this scene.

The tone of the boy's father reflects a state of despair. He said to Jesus: *'If You can do anything, have compassion on us and help us'* (9:22). These words imply that the boy's situation was desperate and hopeless. The parents had done all that they could without any result, and they had now lost faith that a solution was still possible.

Therefore, Jesus asked the father: 'Do you believe?' The father replied: *'Help my unbelief.'* In other words, the father was as if saying, 'Frankly speaking, I have no faith; however, I want to believe. I have lost my faith in the course of this long, exhausting, and devastating journey.'

From this, it is clear that the devil ruins the human soul, isolates it, and then destroys the faith of the people close to the afflicted person in order to eliminate the possibility of restoring peace and hope in God. Consequently, the shadow of death overcasts the whole family.

Faith is the pulse of life. Therefore, when faith is lost, the pulse of life is lost. When faith begins to fade away, this leads to a state similar to that caused by continuous and severe bleeding, meaning the person becomes spiritually dead.

Apostle Mark does not tell us clearly whether the boy actually died during the casting out of the demon or not; he only mentions that many said that the boy was dead.

Because this is a mystical story that comprises special mysteries, the Apostle intended to write with some ambiguity. Mystical stories should not be written in an apparent and revealed way because the mysteries require prepared hearts to receive them. The Holy Spirit then reveals these mysteries to these prepared, fervent, and spiritually sensitive hearts that seek them.

Mysteries are spiritual pearls. At the beginning of His ministry, in the Sermon on the Mount, Jesus said: *'Do not give what is holy to the dogs; nor cast your pearls before swine, lest they trample them under their feet, and turn and tear you in pieces'* (Matthew 7:6). The fallen human heart is animal-like. Therefore, when the pearls are cast before it, it may kick them, meaning it may not appreciate their value. This, in turn, puts such a person under condemnation, and the pearls lose their value. Therefore, the rule is that pearls (mysteries) should be presented in a veiled way. When one with a purified and spiritually sensitive heart approaches these mysteries, they begin to be revealed to him so that he may be nourished by them, live by them, and proclaim their true value to God's people whom God has prepared to hear such precious matters.

Apostle Mark does not mention clearly that the boy died or that he was raised from the dead, yet he used a phrase that is usually used in the Gospels when people are raised from the dead. The Apostle says: *'Jesus took him by the hand and lifted him up, and he arose'* (9:27). Refer to Mark 5:41 (raising Jairus' daughter) and Acts 9:41 (raising Tabitha). This boy was as if dead because the devil had put him to death inwardly. Also, the faith of his father was drained as someone bleeding to death until he reached a point of losing his faith. Therefore, the father was spiritually dead, and the son was actually dead.

What did Jesus do?

Jesus healed the death of faith and the death of the flesh and gave life to both of them.

How and when did Jesus do this?

Jesus did this after proclaiming the Kingdom with power.

As servants of the Lord, we face similar situations in our ministries. These situations will continue as such until the Kingdom of God is proclaimed with power! In other words, these situations will only change when the Kingdom of God is proclaimed in our hearts and we live it out, meaning when Christ reigns within us and becomes King over our lives, conduct, and decisions. The Kingdom will then be proclaimed to the earth (to the world) as well, as explained earlier. When the Kingdom of God begins to be proclaimed to the earth, the manifestations of God's Kingdom will touch the souls. As a result, those possessed with mute evil spirits will speak. The evil spirits will be exposed due to the power of God's Kingdom that is proclaimed around them. Consequently, the faith of the sick people and their families will be revived as they hear the news of God's work in various places—this divine work revives and renews the faith. The powerful work then spreads in the sphere of God's children, and the remembrance of God's name is renewed. As a result, God's Kingdom extends more, as we read in the Book of Acts and in the history of the Church in some generations.

This is the first result of the proclamation of the Kingdom: the people who were descending towards death will be revived, will ascend, and the glory of God and His healing will be manifested in them.

After this event, we read the passage in Mark 9:30–41 where Jesus tells His disciples about His suffering for the second time in this Gospel:

> *The Son of Man is being betrayed into the hands of men, and they will kill Him. And after He is killed, He will rise the third day* (Mark 9:31).

The first time Jesus told His disciples about His suffering (8:31–38), He linked His discourse to *self-denial.* However, this time, He links His discourse about His suffering to the disciples' dispute about *'who would be the greatest'* (Mark 9:34). It is also linked to the issue that the disciples brought up regarding *'someone who does not follow* [them]*'* (Mark 9:38). In the biblical and spiritual language, this issue is called *division, bias,* or *prejudice.*

In this second mention of His suffering, Jesus wanted to highlight that, in addition to self-denial, unity with one another was required. He took a little child and told His disciples that they needed to be like this child, meaning they needed to be simple and deny themselves. But most importantly, it is to be in unity with one another. Therefore, the first step is *self-denial,* and the second step is *unity.*

How is *unity* linked to this second mention of Christ's suffering? How is it the *second step*? How does the crucifixion create unity?

In fact, divisions and biases are mainly caused as a result of *egotism.* Everyone wants to take the glory and honour for himself and hence wants to be on his own, not wanting to be united with the brethren lest he would be hidden and not recognised, while he desires to be well recognised. The cross alone can put to death the ego. Yet, this is a process that happens gradually.

At first, one only needs to constantly resist the ego by reminding himself that he ought to deny himself. When one receives the spirit of self-denial, Jesus will draw near him to lead him to a complete self-denial that will knit him and blend him with the brethren. When this happens, we become a spiritual community—*the body of Christ.* The presence of a body signifies that the Head—the Son of God, is present in the midst (refer to Matthew 18:20). This, in turn, indicates that the Kingdom of God is proclaimed with power. As a result, great signs and miracles will take place, causing the mute evil spirit to flee away and the deadened faith of the boy's father to be revived!

Thus, the manifestation of God's Kingdom with power is illustrated through the healing of the boy who had a mute spirit.

This manifestation requires:

a. Self-denial
b. Avoiding stumbling (Mark 9:42–48)
c. Living a godly life that is seasoned with salt (Mark 9:49, 50)

One of the results of God's Kingdom is that there will be a people of God who are godly, self-denying, and filled with faith and power, who live a life seasoned with salt, and who are united and vigilant over this unity.

Two pictures of stumbling are highlighted in this passage:

- *Causing others to stumble*
- *If your eye causes you to stumble*

According to the verses, if you cause someone to stumble, you are thrown into the sea, whereas if you cause yourself to stumble, you are cast into hell. Being thrown into the sea does not refer to drowning, but it refers to going through the tribulations and turbulences of the sea; the sea refers to the world. Therefore, if you cause someone to stumble, you bring agony, turbulence, and unrest upon yourself. However, if you cause yourself to stumble, this means that you do not value your eternity. This, in turn, means that you are exposing yourself to eternal damnation.

To sum up, we can say that *self-denial* is completed by *unity*. *Unity* means avoiding divisions and bias, avoiding stumbling, and living a godly life that is seasoned with salt.

G. The Picture of God's Kingdom (Mark 10:1–31)

The proclamation of God's Kingdom should be accompanied by the manifestation of the Kingdom picture that the Lord desires to see in His people. This picture was veiled due to the absence of the proclamation of the Kingdom. However, after the proclamation of the Kingdom, this picture ought to be manifested and seen.

The picture of God's Kingdom as highlighted in this part of the Gospel includes:

- The family as a unit of God's Kingdom (Mark 10:1–16):
  - In the likeness of Christ's relationship with His Church
  - The unity between husband and wife

- The children's place in the family

Refer to Ephesians 5:22–6:24

- Leaving earthly things for God's sake (Mark 10:17–31):
  - Coming out of the world and its dominion to be in the sphere of God's Kingdom
  - Leaving the ties of the flesh and earthly riches
  - The more one leaves earthly ties and becomes a sojourner in the world, the more God's Kingdom extends in him and through him.

The disciples accompanied Jesus and were learning from Him in what we may call *the Lord's school* or *the school of the divine Teacher*. Jesus had been taking them gradually along this learning process, teaching them about God's Kingdom, the transfiguration and its results, and now (in this part of the Gospel) about the picture of God's Kingdom.

The opening verse of this chapter highlights where Jesus was on His journey:

> *Then He arose from there and* ***came to the region of Judea*** *by the other side of the Jordan* (Mark 10:1).

Jesus was crossing the river to the east side of the Jordan. Since the region of Judea is mentioned here, this means that He was in the south. [Jesus was actually on a journey that started from the north in Tyre and Sidon until He reached the south in the region of Judea.]

At this moment, He was on the east side of the Jordan. This area is called *Perea*. If Jesus crossed the Jordan to the west, He would be close to Jerusalem and the surrounding areas. The events of the crucifixion were about to take place, and the Passion Week was drawing near; therefore, Jesus was journeying towards Jerusalem to enter the final phase of His Passion and crucifixion.

However, He chose to go from Galilee to Jerusalem through the east side of the Jordan because He wanted to pass by Perea to complete part of His ministry there, which was going to be manifested later, on the day of Pentecost, when God's Kingdom was to be proclaimed to both the Jews and the Gentiles. Thus, at this point, Jesus was in Perea, on the east side of the Jordan, where some Gentiles lived.

The events that the Apostle records here begin with a conversation between Jesus and the Pharisees who asked Jesus about the issue of marriage and divorce.

This is followed by the passage about the children who were brought to Jesus to receive a blessing and how the disciples rebuked those who brought them, but Jesus said: *'Let the little children come to Me, and do not forbid them; for of such is the Kingdom of God'* (10:14).

After this, Apostle Mark takes us to the scene of the *rich young man*. We learn from the Gospel of Luke that this rich young man was a *ruler*. This indicates that he was the ruler of the synagogue in the region of Perea. He came to ask Jesus, *'What shall I do that I may inherit eternal life?'* (10:17).

In response, Jesus pointed out the importance of keeping the commandments. The young man answered and said that he had kept all the commandments from his youth. This reveals that he was sincere. Notice the fine phrase that Apostle Mark uses here, which none of the other Evangelists use. The Apostle wrote that Jesus looked at the man, and He *'loved him'* (10:21). This phrase suggests that Jesus wanted to tell this young man that He knew that he had a sincere heart.

Jesus then continued the conversation with this rich ruler, revealing to him that though he had a sincere heart and had kept the commandments, he had an inner hidden hindrance. Jesus moved gradually in the conversation to help this young man discover this hindrance and then revealed it to him. He began the dialogue by asking the young man about keeping the commandments in order to take him to the following step, which was: *leave everything and follow Me*. Therefore, Jesus said to the rich man:

> *One thing you lack: Go your way, sell whatever you have and give to the poor, and you will have treasure in heaven; and come, take up the cross, and follow Me* (Mark 10:21).

Upon hearing these words, the rich man was saddened and went away sorrowful, because he had great possessions. He refused to leave all his wealth.

The Gospel of Matthew sheds further light on this story by highlighting two phrases that Jesus said to this young rich man:

> *If you want to* ***enter into life, keep the commandments*** (Matthew 19:17).

> *If you want to* ***be perfect****, go,* ***sell what you have*** *and give to the poor, and you will have treasure in heaven; and come, follow Me* (Matthew 19:21).

Based on these words of Jesus, St. Anthony the Great (4th century) sold all his possessions because he desired the path of *perfection*.

Therefore, it is clear that Jesus' discourse with this young rich man comprises two steps:

- If you are only seeking eternal life, keep the commandments, for the commandments are the way to eternal life.
- However, if you seek Me as the Lord of your life, want to be united with Me, and have a perfect and undivided heart

> towards Me—which is the path of perfection—you must empty your heart from every other matter and any idols. There is a hidden idol in your heart: *the love of money.*

After this conversation between Jesus and the rich man, in which Jesus told him to leave everything, bear the cross, and follow Him, the young man went away sorrowful because he had great possessions. Then, Jesus looked at His disciples and said:

> *How hard it is for those who have riches to enter the Kingdom of God!* (Mark 10:23).

The disciples were astonished at His words and wondered whether this meant that anyone who had riches would not have a share in the Kingdom of God! Thus, Jesus explained the difference between *those who **possess** riches* and *those who **trust in** riches.* A person may be rich, yet money may not have a place in his heart, as Abraham for instance. Abraham was rich, yet his heart was filled with love and obedience to God.

Apostle Mark records this story in a way that highlights the difference between *possessing riches* and *trusting in riches* because this is an important distinction.

The disciples were astonished and found these words difficult.

It is difficult for man to *leave,* whether leaving possessions or anything else. The uncircumcised ears find these words difficult. Therefore, if the senses are uncircumcised and the heart is uncircumcised, meaning not cut off from the love of the world, it refuses to leave even trivial matters for God's sake.

When God sees that His people have become attached to certain things, He whispers in their hearts, entreating them to leave these attachments and possessions to be free and completely belonging to Him. These attachments and possessions could be material, meaning money or any riches; they could be emotional, meaning relationships or emotional ties; or they could even be spiritual, meaning a certain ministry, an honour or spiritual status, or excessive attachment to those whom one ministers to. In such cases, God requests the person to *leave*. He may even take that person from one field of ministry to another, so that the person may be in a state of leaving and letting go, not clinging to any matter—even if it comforts him and brings him joy, such as a fruitful ministry or the like.

Thus, various forms of leaving are requested of a believer who desires the path of perfection and being fully united with the Lord. This includes leaving material things, emotional ties and relationships, and even what may appear to be spiritual matters, if the person is too attached to them and clinging to them excessively.

Therefore, in this passage, Peter said to Jesus: *'We have left all and followed You'* (10:28).

Jesus replied:

> *Assuredly, I say to you, there is no one who has left house or brothers or sisters or father or mother or wife or children or lands, **for My sake and the gospel's**, who shall not receive a hundredfold now in this time—houses and brothers and sisters and mothers and children and lands, with persecutions—and in the age to come, eternal life* (Mark 10:29, 30).

Here, Jesus draws our attention to other areas of *leaving* and reveals the purpose of *leaving*.

He generalised leaving to include all wealth and relationships, including the ties of the flesh. The same point about the ties of the flesh is highlighted in the Gospel of Luke. We read: *'If anyone comes to Me and does not hate his father and mother, wife and children, brothers and sisters, yes, and his own life also, he cannot be My disciple'* (Luke 14:26).

Jesus highlights the purpose of *leaving* through the phrase: *for My sake and the gospel's.*[69] This phrase also indicates that the ministry of the gospel requires *leaving*!

Apostle Paul considered himself *'separated to the gospel of God'* (Romans 1:1). If you are a minister of the gospel and desire that the gospel would bear great fruits in your life and ministry, you should make room for it and empty a space for it; it cannot be squeezed amidst your other preoccupations and the things you cling to.

Therefore, leaving includes:

- Leaving riches and wealth
- Leaving the ties of the flesh
- Leaving all earthly ties, whether houses, fields, family, friends, and so on. In this passage, the houses and fields refer to any earthly ties and possessions.

After discussing the events and scenes of this chapter, we can now outline the main ideas and purpose of this part and the connection between the successive scenes mentioned in this chapter.

The chapter begins by presenting a picture of God's Kingdom which is the picture of the family as a unit of God's Kingdom. There should be inseparable unity between the husband and wife and there should be no divorce since this unity is in the likeness of the unity between Christ and His Church or Christ and the human soul as a Bridegroom and a bride.

---

69 Mark 10:29. Note that Apostle Mark is the only Evangelist who mentions this phrase due to his great love for the gospel!

The Kingdom should be manifested in the family as the first small unit of God's Kingdom. God reigns over this small unit when the husband and wife are united in an inseparable unity, meaning they do not have the option or thought of separation. This unity is completed by the offspring who are an extension of God's Kingdom in this first small unit. The children are also considered the Kingdom school where the parents learn many matters pertaining to their relationship with the heavenly Father through their relationship with their children.

A parent once said that he suffered from a sense of guilt; thus, whenever he would make a mistake, he would think that God was angry with him. Then, one day, God drew near him during prayer and spoke to his heart, saying:

Don't your children disobey you at times and upset you; how do you feel towards them? Do you reject them?

This person replied:

Of course not, I do not reject them; they are my children; I may get upset by their conduct at times, while, at other times, I just feel that it is okay, they will soon grow out of that behaviour. But I never reject them; I continually love them.

The Lord then said:

Is it possible that you would have such love for your children, while I, your heavenly Father, would not have a similar steadfast love towards you?

After this revelation which was derived from his relationship with his children, this man's problem with the sense of guilt ended.

The parents who pay attention to these lessons and revelations will notice that as their children grow up, they themselves also grow in their relationship with the heavenly Father. They increasingly taste and experience the Fatherhood and Motherhood of God.

Thus, both the marital life and the relationship with the children are considered a divine school in which the parents learn and grow in the matters of God's Kingdom.

As the children grow up, the form of this unit of God's Kingdom progresses and extends. The children begin to have spiritual fellowship with their parents. Then, they receive a divine commission. This indeed brings joy to their parents. Then, when they leave their parents' home and have their own family, this family will be a further extension of God's Kingdom. Thus, the first unit of the family continues to extend to include more families until these families become a small church, which then grows to be a big church in an area or in a city.

However, this picture can only be manifested in this form if we learn the true ties of the spirit. This means that the biological father should be a biological and spiritual father for his children. If the father is a spiritual person, he will teach his children not only manners, cultures, and human sciences, but he will also be keen on teaching them matters pertaining to God's Kingdom. If the parents do this, God's Kingdom will extend and will be manifested. It begins as small units that grow and extend, becoming one church under the care of the fatherhood of a priest or pastor. This is the desire of God's heart.

Biblically speaking, parents who fail to teach their children God's commandments and His Word means that they are unable to complete the divine commission requested of them:

> *Now this is the commandment, and these are the statutes and judgments which the Lord your God has commanded to teach you, that you may observe them in the land which you are crossing*

> *over to possess, that you may fear the Lord your God, to keep all His statutes and His commandments which I command you,* ***you and your son and your grandson,*** *all the days of your life, and that your days may be prolonged. Therefore hear, O Israel, and be careful to observe it, that it may be well with you, and that you may multiply greatly as the Lord God of your fathers has promised you—'a land flowing with milk and honey.' Hear, O Israel: The Lord our God, the Lord is one! You shall love the Lord your God with all your heart, with all your soul, and with all your strength. And these words which I command you today shall be in your heart.* ***You shall teach them diligently to your children,*** *and shall talk of them when you sit in your house, when you walk by the way, when you lie down, and when you rise up. You shall bind them as a sign on your hand, and they shall be as frontlets between your eyes. You shall write them on the doorposts of your house and on your gates* (Deuteronomy 6:1–9).

After presenting this picture of the family, its members, their relationship, and the importance of growing and moving forward in God's will and His Kingdom, the Gospel sheds light on the ultimate purpose of this family as a unit in God's Kingdom. The purpose can be summed up in one phrase: *eternal life*. Remember the question that the young rich man asked the Lord: *'What must I do to inherit eternal life?'* (10:17). What is the way to this eternal life? Again, the answer can be put in one word, derived from Christ's words to this rich young man: *leave* (10:21). The more I leave, the more I am given; the more I become a sojourner in this world, the more God's Kingdom extends in me and through me.

Notice how the passages are all connected to convey the spiritual, revelatory meaning that we ought to perceive as we read the Word of God and seek depth and revelation.

Thus, to sum up this point, we can say that one of the pictures of God's Kingdom is that of a family that lives for the sake of God's Kingdom and serves God's Kingdom, always fixing their eyes on and awaiting eternal life.

Not only this, but there is also another dimension which we need to be mindful of. In order to reflect a true picture of God's Kingdom, the family, or rather the church, which is a bigger family, ought to be adorned with familial warmth and love. Because the Church has lost many of its treasures and riches over the centuries due to the divisions, we often see parishioners sitting or standing next to each other while not even knowing those next to them; they have become strangers to one another. This matter alone is sufficient to make the Church lack the reflection of the true Kingdom picture!

The whole congregation ought to be one united, reconciled family in true love. When they come together in unity and reconciliation, the Holy Spirit pours upon them deeper love towards one another and renews their love: '*That the love with which You loved Me may be in them, and I in them*' (John 17:26).

The purpose of establishing a church in a certain area is that the congregation in this area may be one spiritual family living as a community, having a shared spiritual life in love. Familial warmth and love are important characteristics of the Kingdom family.

Thus, the two dimensions are:

- The unit of the family is a picture of God's Kingdom.
- This Kingdom family ought to be adorned with familial warmth, unity, and love.

Spiritual gatherings in the homes help preserve the familial warmth and allow the members to worship together. Gathering together in the church ties the members to their local church and allows them to receive the teaching from one secure source.

Apostle Mark concludes his account about serving God's Kingdom with this elaborate and well-connected picture of God's Kingdom. Since at this point Jesus was concluding His ministry as He was drawing close to the crucifixion, this is the last chapter in this Gospel that discusses God's Kingdom and its ministry. This theme ends at 10:31, and a new theme, crucifixion and redemption, begins at 10:32 until the end of the Gospel. This will be the theme of our discussion in the next point.

2. CHRIST'S REDEMPTION (MARK 10:32–MARK 16)

The first ten chapters of the Gospel of Mark focus on ministry, highlighting important principles of serving God's Kingdom. Now, we come to the second part of the Gospel, which focuses on redemption and crucifixion.

Main points of the second part of the Gospel of Mark:

A. Going up to Jerusalem (Mark 10:32–52)

B. Inside Jerusalem (Mark 11–13)

C. The manifestation of redemption through the crucifixion and resurrection (Mark 14–16)

A. Going Up to Jerusalem (Mark 10:32–52)

Three main steps or characteristics are required to go up to Jerusalem:

- The cross (10:32–34)
- Self-sacrifice (10:35–45)
- Throwing aside the garment (10:46–52)

The purpose of this part is to learn some truths pertaining to our personal spiritual life. These truths focus on two main aspects:

- Christ, the Saviour, with whom we unite
- The path of salvation as containing living signs that ought to be followed

As we mentioned, this part of the Gospel focuses on *going up to Jerusalem*. What is Jerusalem and what does it represent? It is the spiritual capital of Judea.

What then is the spiritual significance of Jerusalem, and how can we benefit from this?

Jerusalem is *the city of the great King*[70] and the centre of God's presence in His house. The house of God, which is equivalent to the Church, is in Jerusalem. It contains the temple. According to the Jews, the house of God is the place of God's presence. Because of this, Jerusalem is geographically situated on a high place, a hill, since God dwells on high, as the Scriptures say.[71] Thus, when we read here that Jesus and the disciples were *going up to Jerusalem*, this indicates that they were actually ascending one of the small mountains in Jerusalem—the mountain of Zion.

Throughout this study, we have seen how Apostle Mark often directs his lens to certain scenes and focuses on them for a certain purpose or to convey a certain meaning. Therefore, here the Apostle directs his lens to three scenes or signs to highlight that whoever desires to draw near the place of God's presence (Jerusalem) and enter into fellowship with God must pay attention to and observe these three practical signs.

The Apostle wrote his Gospel to the Romans, who were estranged from God, in order to lead them to God's path and help them know that this path has clear, specific, and practical steps. Therefore, he highlights that three steps are required in order to *go up* to Jerusalem, meaning to live close to God and not far away from Him. These steps or characteristics are attainable by the grace of God, and when they are obeyed, they truly transform the lives of those who obey them and transform their relationship with God.

However, it is important to note that we ought to learn the true spiritual path from the Word of God in order to live out our

70 Matthew 5:35
71 Psalm 113:5; Isaiah 57:15

spiritual life according to God's mind and enter into the depths of the Word of God. Unfortunately, believers often live out spiritual matters based on their own thoughts and impressions or on what they hear from other people, and hence, many spiritual matters in their lives may be mere human points of view. However, as we have said, the true spiritual path has to be based on and derived from the Word of God. The Early Fathers of the Church understood the Word of God well because they lived it out and entered its depths. Thus, they were able to interpret and explain how the Bible could be practically lived out.

The three steps for *going up to Jerusalem* are:

- The cross
- Self-sacrifice
- Throwing aside the garment

▪ The Cross (10:32–34)

In order to go up to Jerusalem one ought to accept the path of the cross, meaning accept various types of suffering.

In this part, Apostle Mark refers to the Passion of Christ for the third time in his Gospel:

> *Now they were on the road,* ***going up to Jerusalem****, and Jesus was going before them; and they were amazed. And as they followed they were afraid. Then He took the twelve aside again and began to tell them the things that would happen to Him: "Behold, we are going up to Jerusalem, and the Son of Man will be betrayed to the chief priests and to the scribes; and they will condemn Him to death and deliver Him to the Gentiles; and they will mock Him, and scourge Him, and spit on Him, and kill Him. And the third day He will rise again"* (Mark 10:32–34).

Each time the Apostle mentions the Passion of Christ, he focuses on a certain angle. In the first mention of Christ's suffering (Mark 8:31), he focuses on the suffering caused by the religious leaders or the small circle. In the second mention of Christ's suffering (Mark 9:31), the Apostle highlights that these sufferings can occur from the larger circle. In the third mention of Christ's suffering (Mark 10:33, 34), the Apostle highlights a further step, which is: *being handed over to the Gentiles.* The emphasis here is on *being put to public shame and disgrace.*

Practically speaking, whoever desires to draw closer to God faces the battles of the devil, who wars against him in this same way or pattern. We often look at these battles in a general way, but if we perceive their nature and significance in a more specific way, we can be steadfast in them and overcome them by God's grace.

Based on this revelation in the Gospel of Mark, we understand that when we begin to draw closer to God and desire to ascend upwards in our fellowship with God, we face mockery and ridicule. This may surprise us or even cause us to stumble, but if we understand the divine revelation conveyed through this Gospel, we will perceive that this is the path of the cross that leads us closer to the Crucified One!

Mockery or ridicule may come from the inner circle, meaning from the children of God or even some servants of the Lord, as we have seen in the mockery of *the Pharisees,* or it may come from the outer circle, meaning the non-believers, as we read here about the mockery coming from *the Gentiles.*

This may cause us to stumble and even complain to God, saying: 'Does following You involve such disgrace and mockery?' We may also be astonished that the mockery comes from people we do not expect it from. However, reading this part of the Gospel and perceiving the divine revelation in it helps us understand that this is the nature of the path of ascent to be in closer fellowship with God; it is the path of the cross that we must accept and bear if we desire to ascend the mountain of fellowship with the Lord. This, in turn, helps us to be free from people's views which can hinder us from ascending.

Being free from the opinions of others is generally an important spiritual principle and is one of the characteristics of a spiritually mature person. If the person is enslaved to people's opinions, this is a sign of spiritual immaturity. Conversely, if the person is free from people's opinions and comments, and all that matters to him is God's mind and will, this is a sign of spiritual maturity that leads the person closer to God and allows him to experience true human and spiritual freedom. In 1 Corinthians 7:23, we read: *'You were bought at a price; do not become slaves of men.'* Thus, the Scripture stresses the importance of being free from people and from desiring to please them, and being instead slaves to God and fulfilling His will.[72]

Being enslaved to people is spiritually harmful because it is often hidden and can take various forms, damaging one's personality and causing the person to lose his inner peace. Being close to God frees us from the dominion of people and from this kind of slavery! When we draw close to God, God's grace forms a sort of insulation between us and others. Thus, neither mockery nor coercion enslaves us or affects us.

The real cause of being enslaved to others is the attitude and response of the person himself when he allows himself to fall under the influence and effect of what others say. As a result of this attitude, the person finds himself disturbed by people's harshness and

---

72 The Scriptures also speak about freedom from sin: *'Therefore if the Son makes you free, you shall be free indeed'* (John 8:36), and freedom from Satan and his enslavement, referred to in the story of Pharaoh and the exodus from Egypt (Exodus 1:14; 3:7–10).

mockery towards him, or at times, he even begs for their kindness. When this person is praised, he feels that he needs this praise, and hence, he finds himself willing to completely submit to the person who praised him to always be praised by him. Similarly, if this person is reproached, he is disturbed and confused, and thus, he withdraws, thinking to himself that he should try to please the one who reproached him so that he would not reproach him again, because he is unable to cope with reproach. All this shows that the person himself is responsible for his attitude or response to what others do or say.

Do we seek to please people or to please God?

In this context, Apostle Paul says:

> *For do I now persuade men, or God? Or do I seek to please men? For if I still pleased men, I would not be a bondservant of Christ* (Galatians 1:10).

To sum up, we can say that the first step or characteristic to go up to Jerusalem, meaning to draw closer to God, is *the cross*. The cross here signifies accepting suffering. The suffering referred to here is the suffering that comes from the mockery of those who reject the spiritual life. When a person begins to have closer fellowship with God and a desire to draw closer to God, he may face opposition from such people, whether through their mocking him or giving him false advice, because a sincere, dedicated life to God is often rejected and subjected to mockery. This may continue until grace transfigures this person's life, and then his life becomes a testimony. The Scripture says: *'Yes, and all who desire to live godly in Christ Jesus will suffer persecution'* (2 Timothy 3:12). In most cases, this persecution begins when the person takes steps towards living a more sincere and earnest life with God and continues until the grace is manifested and transfigures him. During this time, the person may be mocked, and he needs to be prepared to bear this kind of suffering. If the person accepts this suffering, he goes up to Jerusalem and is close to God's heart! However, if the person stumbles and resists the suffering, his ascent may be hindered or delayed; he may even halt at a certain level in the spiritual life, or he may fluctuate between ascending and descending.

This step could be best described as a hill that has a slope and a peak. If the person stands on the slope, he is subject to rolling downwards. He may try to go up again, but he may still continually fluctuate between going up for some time and going down again. However, if he continues to ascend without stopping, he will eventually reach the top of the hill, where he finds a flat-levelled highland above the level of the world.

This is a difficult stage. It is the first step in going up to Jerusalem!

▪ Self-Sacrifice (10:35–45)

The second step or characteristic of going up to Jerusalem is highlighted through the story of the sons of Zebedee (Mark 10:35–45). James and John ask Jesus to grant them that they might sit, one on His right hand and the other on His left, in His glory.

[In the Gospel of Matthew (20:20), it is mentioned that the mother of the sons of Zebedee made this request. According to historical accounts, their mother was the cousin of the Virgin Mary, according to the flesh. Because of this kinship, she most likely wanted to request prestigious positions for her sons for when the reign of Jesus came, which she imagined to be an earthly reign like that of David, Solomon, or any other king.]

Hearing this request, the other ten disciples were greatly displeased and indignant, and as if they wanted to say, 'Why this favouritism?'

But Jesus said to them:

> *Whoever desires to become great among you shall be your servant. And whoever of you desires to be first shall be slave of all. For even the Son of Man did not come to be served, but to serve, and to give His life a ransom for many* (Mark 10:43–45).

Here, Jesus was telling His disciples to forget about this idea of wanting to be great and forget about all these human conflicts. Immediately before this passage, He said to His disciples: *'You know that those who are considered rulers over the Gentiles lord it over them, and their great ones exercise authority over them. Yet it shall not be so among you'* (Mark 10:42, 43a). In other words, *if you desire to go up to Jerusalem, you need to determine in your heart that you will not allow these human struggles to hinder you. Therefore, you need not only to deny yourselves, but you also need to sacrifice yourselves.* Remember that we mentioned earlier that self-denial is the first step in following the Crucified One, but there is a further step that must follow, which is sacrifice.

Denying oneself is a passive attitude, whereas sacrificing oneself is an active attitude.

Self-denial can be passive in the sense that one persuades himself not to be bothered or concerned by what others may do to him or take from him. He as if tells himself: 'Let people take what they want and let them do as they please; I have no problem with that. I will not bother myself with these matters.' There is a clear sense of pain and agony in these words, as if the person is trying to force or persuade himself to respond in this way.

However, *self-sacrifice* is a different attitude, where one seems to say: 'What do you want to take from me? Do you want to take my honour and position? Take anything you want; I find pleasure in giving and sacrificing.'

With self-denial, the person may be crying from within, saying: 'Enough! I can no longer bear it; I cannot cope with people treading on me in such a way!' However, with self-sacrifice, the person experiences being as though in a completely different place; he is no longer down in the valley, oppressed by people and being under their control, but is rather on the top of the hill, in Jerusalem. He has *ascended to Jerusalem*.

Christ Himself was exposed to mockery, persecution, crucifixion, and shame; however, He was always lifted up.

When Jesus was silent and did not respond to Pilate's accusations, during His trial before the crucifixion, Pilate said to Jesus: *'Are You not speaking to me? Do You not know that I have power to crucify You, and power to release You?'* (John 19:10). In other words, Pilate was in a way telling Jesus to seize this opportunity and reply in order to win his (Pilate's) favour and approval.

However, Jesus said to him:

> *You could have no power at all against Me unless it had been given you* ***from above****. Therefore the one who delivered Me to you has the greater sin* (John 19:11).

The phrase *from above* means *from the Father*. Jesus wanted to highlight that there was a higher authority, the authority of God, the Creator of the universe.

What does being up in Jerusalem practically indicate?

When the person is *down in the valley*, he sees the people around him and what they do. The world is full of struggles, evil, and conspiracies; everyone wants to tread on the other and deceive the other. This is all a person is able to see when he is down in the valley. However, when the person *ascends* and eventually reaches Jerusalem, the city of the Great King and the place of

God's presence, the first thing that happens is that when he looks down, everything then seems tiny and small and of no value. The second thing that happens is that he no longer finds the people around him running about and panting, each trying to be the best, because all who are present in this higher place are of one mind and one spirit. Furthermore, this person will then look around and know that the closest Person to him is the Father, the Great King. Thus, he then sees all the scenes as they truly are. Consequently, all the things that he previously cared about when he was in the valley no longer have any value to him! He will be surprised that he had even once cared about these matters before. He will at this point perceive that his life is controlled by God and that God is the One who has the say in all matters, not human beings.

When the person is *down in the valley,* he is often unable to see well. The people around him obscure his vision and hide God's face from him; thus, he thinks that his fate is in the people's hands. Therefore, he tries to please some, reproaches some, and is afraid of some. All he sees are these people and he thinks that they have control over his fate.

However, when this person *ascends to Jerusalem,* leaving all these matters behind, he perceives that all the people that he once thought could influence his fate and that he once cared so much about are in reality merely poor souls and are only human beings like him; *God holds their breath in His hands,* and hence their life may end at any minute, as Daniel said to King Belshazzar (Daniel 5:23, 30).

Therefore, when Pilate said to Jesus that His fate was in his hands and he could crucify Him or release Him, Jesus did not remain silent this time. Jesus clarified that this was not the case and that His fate was not in Pilate's hands at all. Thus, Jesus replied saying:

'You could have no power at all against Me unless it had been given you ***from above****'* (John 19:11).

Jesus wanted to emphasise that the *One above, the Father,* was the only One who decided in this matter, not Pilate, for everything is decided *'by the determined purpose and foreknowledge of God'* (Acts 2:23). Therefore, if Pilate decided to crucify Jesus, it would not be Pilate's decision but God's. Pilate was no more than a servant of God, and God guided him according to His word and command. In other words, Jesus was as if saying to Pilate: 'Though you neither know God nor see Him, when He says His word, you will find yourself signing off on it. However, if God binds this word, no matter what you try to do, you will neither be able to sign off on it nor even utter it!'

How wonderful it is to live with this faith and vision! This is the true meaning of going up to Jerusalem.

When the person ascends and goes up to Jerusalem, his life becomes free from the struggles and conflicts related to the world, money, people, status, prestige, and the like, which are dust and temporary matters that will perish. In short, his life becomes free from all that is false and vain. Hence, one's life is set aright and connected with what is above. This, in turn, means that one's fate is in God's hands from A to Z, including his life, days, family, and everything. Consequently, his humanity becomes completely connected and united with God. If the person lives down in the valley, absorbed in earthly matters, he remains a mere human being, whereas, if he ascends upwards, he truly becomes a *partaker of the divine nature* (2 Peter 1:4). Down in the valley, he remains a human being who cannot but struggle with others, and *only the strongest survive,* as they say. However, up in Jerusalem, the human tactics, struggles, and rules that are full of injustice and oppression do not exist. This is because the One above is the Righteous, the

Just, and the Good, whose mercy endures forever! Since my fate is in His hands, my soul rests at peace.

If one desires to ascend and live a life from above, he first needs to discern where he is, whether he is in the valley or in Jerusalem. If he is in the valley, there is nothing in the valley except struggles and convulsions (as we read in the story of the epileptic boy in Mark 9). The struggles are related to human beings, while the convulsions are related to evil spirits. If the devil gets hold of a person, he convulses him, meaning he completely ruins and destroys him, as we read in Mark 9:26: *convulsed him violently* (NIV). However, when the person ascends, he becomes free from the evil spirits and the demons because he becomes connected with God and bound to Him. Being *partakers of the divine nature* means that God grants us to share in His life and He binds us to Him so that we may live above, in the heavenly places:

> *Which He worked in Christ when **He raised Him from the dead and seated Him at His right hand in the heavenly places,** far above all principality and power and might and dominion, and every name that is named, not only in this age but also in that which is to come. And He put all things under His feet, and gave Him to be head over all things to the church* (Ephesians 1:20–22).

> *And raised us up together, and made us sit together in the heavenly places in Christ Jesus* (Ephesians 2:6).

▪ Throwing Aside the Garment (10:46–52)

The third step or characteristic of going up to Jerusalem is to throw the cloak aside.

The cloak has a spiritual significance that can be perceived from Scripture. It is an outer robe which one wears and which others can see. Thus, it refers to one's outer, visible conduct. It can hinder the person and cause him to stumble; therefore, one may want to take it off. From this, we understand that the cloak refers to earthly and worldly preoccupations, worries, and entanglements.

According to the old Jewish tradition, the Jewish people would wear a loose garment and then wear a sleeveless cloak that was open at the front on top of it. Based on this, Jesus said, in the Sermon on the Mount: '*If anyone wants to sue you and take away your tunic, let him have your cloak also*' (Matthew 5:40). This attitude signifies that one does not want to be hindered or delayed by anything; he is running towards a certain aim and does not want his feet to be held up from reaching their goal by someone holding onto his tunic or cloak. Thus, he leaves both the tunic and cloak to ascend the hill of Jerusalem and live close to God's heart, for he is called to be up in Jerusalem, not down in the valley. Christ has lifted us up and granted us this ascent through His cross, for it is written: '*And I, if I am lifted up from the earth* [meaning lifted up on the cross], *will draw all peoples to Myself*' (John 12:32).

Jesus was lifted up on the cross for our sake, not only to redeem us and forgive our sins, but also to place us up in the heavenly places, and lift us up by His resurrection (Ephesians 2:6). Our place is up in the heavenly places; we are the ones who bring ourselves down below to the valley.

What prevents us from going up?

It can be the cloak, the ego, or running away from the cross. These are the true reasons that prevent us from going up or hinder our ascent.

The cloak of earthly entanglements can hinder the person because it can numb him and blind his eyes, causing him to be unable to discern whether he lives for God or for the world. Such a person needs to learn the signs of the spiritual path from the Word of

God and keep them in his heart. God's Word has authority over the mind and conscience, and it produces in the person obedience and the ability to walk with God despite people's opposing views or one's personal preferences, which can be deceitful.

The ego is also a factor that can hinder one from going up to Jerusalem.

Another factor that may hinder one from ascending may be *the desire to avoid the path of bearing the cross*, meaning one's desire to run away from the suffering that may occur when one follows the Lord.

Some people falsely worry that following the Lord may lead them to face more tribulations! When I was a student in university, my friends and I had great zeal for ministry, so we would invite our fellow students to our youth meetings. One of the students in our year level always refused the invitation and always came up with excuses. At that time, we had great zeal and fervent love for God, and it was painful to see someone deprived of the blessing of these spiritual gatherings. Thus, one day, we visited this fellow student and asked him why he always refused to come to the meetings. We explained that we felt that he had been missing out on great blessings, and we all needed his presence with us. This student explained that each time he went to a meeting, a catastrophe would happen in his life during the same week. For instance, a member of his family would fall seriously ill, or he would break his leg, or anything of the like. He went on to say that when he had asked about this matter, he was told that this was natural because the Scripture says, *'many are the afflictions of the righteous'* (Psalm 34:19). We responded by telling him that this was only half of the verse and that the verse actually says: *'Many are the afflictions of the righteous, but the Lord delivers him out of them all'* (Psalm 34:19). As a result, this person began to attend the meetings again and his problem was resolved because the truth sets us free: *'And you shall know the truth, and the truth shall make you free'* (John 8:32).

B. Inside Jerusalem (Mark 11–13)

Jerusalem is the City of the Great King and the place of God's presence; thus, it refers to a life that is close to God's heart.

We have been journeying with Apostle Mark as he takes us step by step from one scene to the other to highlight specific points and principles. As we draw closer to the crucifixion and resurrection, these scenes are about to end. Only one last scene remains before the events of the crucifixion begin.

After describing the scene of going up to Jerusalem, the Apostle wants to draw our attention to important characteristics that those who go up to Jerusalem ought to understand. Therefore, he highlights two main points that ought to be observed inside Jerusalem:

1. Stand firm to avoid slipping and descending or going downhill
2. Perceive one's responsibilities in Jerusalem, how to live, and what life is like inside Jerusalem

Remember that these scenes take place in Jerusalem not as a geographical place only, but Jerusalem also reflects and symbolises an important aspect of our spiritual journey. Jerusalem symbolises the believer's relationship with God. It does not refer to advanced spiritual levels, as we may think,[73] but to the lives of those who wish to live close to God's heart in sincerity and truth. This life is available to anyone; however, we ought to learn its characteristics, perceive them well, and be steadfast in them.

73 In fact, this way of thinking causes us to remain at a weak and dry level in our spiritual life.

Therefore, in this part of his Gospel, Apostle Mark focuses his lens on some scenes that provide practical steps for living inside Jerusalem, as we will explain.

We can thus outline the framework and main points of this part of the Gospel as follows:

In order to live in Jerusalem, we ought to:

1. Stand firm in the life of Jerusalem

The signs of standing firm in the life in Jerusalem are:

- Jesus is my King: Blessed is He who comes in the Name of the Lord[74] (Mark 11:1–11)
- Consecration and its fruits: cleansing the temple, cursing the fig tree (Mark 11:12–33)

2. Perceive the characteristics of life in Jerusalem to be able to continue in this life—a life close to God's heart—and understand its responsibilities

These characteristics are highlighted through Christ's discourses about:

- The vineyard and its responsibility (Mark 12:1–12)
- Rendering to Caesar the things that are Caesar's and to God the things that are God's (Mark 12:13–17)
- The resurrection of the dead (Mark 12:18–27)
- The disposition of the heart (Mark 12:28–44)
- The second coming (Mark 13)

1. Stand Firm in the Life of Jerusalem

The signs of standing firm in the life of Jerusalem are:

74 Mark 11:9

- ***Jesus is My King: Blessed is He who comes in the Name of the Lord (Mark 11:1–11)***

This point is highlighted through the scene of Christ's entry into Jerusalem. Notice the interesting analogy between this scene and the scene that precedes it—the scene of healing blind Bartimaeus.

In the story of Bartimaeus, we read:

> ***Throwing his cloak aside,*** *he jumped to his feet and came to Jesus* (Mark 10:50, NIV).

Then, in the scene of Christ's entry into Jerusalem, we read:

> *Many people* ***spread their cloaks*** *on the road* (Mark 11:8, NIV).

Thus, we see that the blind man throws aside his cloak while the people spread their cloaks on the road. The blind man's cloak refers to the cloak of earthly worries and entanglements, as explained earlier, whereas the people's cloaks represent the cloak of consecration and submission to God.

As mentioned earlier, the cloak refers to one's outer conduct. Therefore, from these two stories, we understand that there are matters that one must lay aside, put an end to, and say of, 'Enough of these matters that estrange me from Christ and from eternal life because they represent the cloak of earthly worries, entanglements, and hindrances'. On the other hand, the cloak of consecration represents a conduct that reflects that we are truly God's children and we submit to Him. When our conduct is pleasing to God, it means that we have put our cloaks under Christ's feet, and hence, our lives truly belong to Him. This conduct is reflected in the procession of Christ's entry into Jerusalem and highlights its spiritual significance.

Some people spread their cloaks before Jesus, while others spread palm branches. In those days, this was the usual practice of welcoming a king. People would hail the king by waving palm branches as a sign of respect and welcome. They would also spread their cloaks at the feet of a king to express honour and as a sign of inviting this king to step on their clothes. In fact, spreading their clothes before the king to step on was a proclamation from the people of their desire to submit to the king.

Therefore, when Christ entered Jerusalem, the people spread their clothes and waved palm branches, illustrating that they were celebrating Him as a King. They also shouted: *'Blessed is he who comes in the name of the Lord!'*

What is the spiritual significance behind this act and the cries of the people?

Jesus is not an earthly king but a King who reigns over the hearts to lead them to His complete salvation. Therefore, the people were shouting, *'Hosanna'*, meaning 'Save us'. In other words, it is as if they were saying: 'We submit our lives to You; may Your salvation come upon our lives.'

The more we submit to the Lord, the more we experience the effect and fruits of His salvific work. This, in turn, helps us rid ourselves of the many opposing things that hinder our fellowship with God and hinder His purposes for our lives. These hindrances can be sins in our lives, problems, evil people, difficult circumstances, or anything else. It is possible to get rid of them all because, as the Epistle to the Hebrews states, Christ is able to *'save to the uttermost those who come to God through Him'*.[75]

This highlights the purpose of Jesus becoming King over our lives and the significance of the phrase *'Blessed is He who comes in the name of the Lord'*.

---

75 Hebrews 7:25

• *Consecration and Its Fruits: Cleansing the Temple, Cursing the Fig Tree (Mark 11:12–33)*

This is the second sign of standing firm in Jerusalem.

When Jesus entered Jerusalem, He performed two important things: He cursed the fig tree and cleansed the temple.

At first, He entered the temple on Sunday, looked at it and carefully examined it, and then went back to Bethany. In Luke 19:41, we read that Jesus wept over Jerusalem because of what it had become and its fast-approaching destruction. Then, the next day, as He walked with His disciples, He spoke to them about faith and its fruits (Mark 11:20–26).

What is the spiritual significance of this part of the Gospel, and how is it connected to the previous scene?

When Jesus becomes King over our lives, He seeks to find fruits. However, we cannot be fruitful unless our inner temple is cleansed and purified and has nothing of the world's corruption. If the corruption of the world enters into our inner temple, our vine will wither and will be barren of fruits.

Jesus always seeks the fruits of our calling because every believer must bear fruits for God's Kingdom. The required fruits vary from one person to the other based on one's calling. One person may be required to bear fruits of worship, while another fruits of acts of mercy. One may have a ministry in the church and be required to bear the fruits of this particular ministry, while another may have a role in serving the Lord in the world among non-believers and be required to bring forth the fruits of this work. Therefore, there are various kinds of callings and various kinds of fruits,[76] but the principle remains that one must glorify

76 1 Corinthians 12:4–6

the Lord in whatever role he is entrusted with, and not glorify his ego or seek vainglory. Also, the principle always holds that one will not bear any fruits unless his life is cleansed from the corruption of the world. Each generation has its distinct form of corruption, which shapes the people of this particular generation. For this reason, the Scriptures exhort us not to conform to the world but to be transformed by the renewing of our minds (Romans 12:2).

If one keeps his life from corruption, one's life becomes fruitful. Daniel the Prophet presents a clear example in this respect. The Scripture says about him:

> *But Daniel purposed in his heart that he would not defile himself with the portion of the king's delicacies, nor with the wine which he drank* (Daniel 1:8).

When Daniel and his three friends were appointed a daily provision of the king's delicacies and the wine he drank, which were prohibited according to Jewish law, Daniel chose to adhere to the law and keep himself clean and pure. He and his friends, being in captivity and these being the king's orders, could have chosen to eat whatever was offered to them. However, when faced with this challenge, Daniel chose to adhere to the law and was thus granted favour in the eyes of the chief of the eunuchs, who agreed to give them vegetables instead of the daily provision appointed by the king.

The fruit of Daniel's choice and his attitude of keeping himself pure and clean, despite the king's orders, was that God granted him special wisdom and the gift of interpreting visions and dreams. Daniel did not have these gifts before, but they were indeed the fruit of a holy life that remained holy despite the uncleanness and filthiness of the world around him.

Fasting actually purifies the soul and clears the mind. When one controls or limits his food intake, not for the sake of food itself, but to focus on worship and be fervent in spirit, one's soul is illumined, his mind becomes clear, and God grants him various gifts.

God granted Daniel these gifts of wisdom and interpretation because He knew that Daniel would glorify God through these gifts. This was manifested in Daniel interpreting the dream of King Nebuchadnezzar, which all the magicians, the astrologers, the sorcerers, and the Chaldeans failed to interpret.

Because Daniel kept his inner temple clean, he bore the fruit of wisdom, through which he testified to the king about God and His mysteries. When Daniel told the king about the dream and its interpretation, the arrogant king bowed down and said that there was no other God but the God of Daniel:

> *Then King Nebuchadnezzar fell on his face, prostrate before Daniel ... and said, "Truly your God is the God of gods, the Lord of kings, and a revealer of secrets, since you could reveal this secret"* (Daniel 2:46, 47).

When we follow the life of this king in the books of Scripture, we see how his life was transformed from paganism into faith in the God of Daniel. Thus, Daniel, a mere captive, was able to make a pagan, stubborn, arrogant, and tough king—who was the emperor of the world at that time—believe in the true God. The key was that he kept himself holy and pure and refused to break the commandment. How great the things that can be accomplished by obeying God are! Obedience to God allows a captive to transform an emperor from paganism to believing in the true God.

Daniel did not do much to accomplish this great mission! He only obeyed God and kept His commandments. Today, believers, on the other hand, often want to evangelise and bring souls to Christ while eating of the world's delicacies and drinking of its unclean drinks, unaware of the importance of being separate and set apart for the Lord. The reference here is not to material food and drink but to the uncleanness of the world that may be offered to us. These types of food and drink may be offered to us, for instance, through unchaste or impure relationships. If we do not refuse them, our lives become darkened. Then, when the time comes and we begin to bear witness to the Lord, we find our testimony ineffective. The reason for this is that our lives are darkened and our words are dead, coming only from our lips, not from a holy life. On the other hand, a simple person who obeys the commandments and keeps his inner temple clean, when he says a few simple words, people will be convicted and repent instantaneously, desiring to know the God of this poor person. The key here is that a pure, holy life bears witness to the Lord and leads people to repentance much more than evangelism and preaching that are not supported and accompanied by a holy life!

2. Characteristics of Life in Jerusalem

Chapters 12 and 13 highlight five characteristics of life in Jerusalem that are reflected in the discourses of Jesus with His disciples during the week before His crucifixion (Mark 12) and also in His discourse about the second coming and the signs of the end times (Mark 13). We need to understand the spiritual significance of these discourses to perceive the characteristics of life in Jerusalem.

The five discourses are:

a. The parable of the vineyard and the vinedressers (Mark 12:1–12)
b. A question about whether to pay taxes to Caesar (Mark 12:13–17)
c. The resurrection of the dead (Mark 12:18–27)

d. Disputes that reveal the inner state of the heart and its relevance to our relationship with God (Mark 12:28–44)
e. The second coming and the required watchfulness and vigilance (Mark 13)

A brief overview of these five discourses

a. The parable of the vineyard and the vinedressers

Through this parable, Jesus highlights the following points:

- The vineyard refers to Israel in general (Isaiah 5)
- This vineyard has become fruitless
- The responsibility of the vinedressers, meaning the scribes, the priests, the Pharisees, and the religious people in charge, who rejected Christ who came to bring them salvation: *the chief cornerstone which the builders rejected* (Mark 12:10)

b. Is it lawful to pay taxes to Caesar, or not?

The Pharisees hypocritically and cunningly asked Jesus this question to set a trap for Him. If His reply suggested that taxes should not be paid to Caesar, it meant that He was against Caesar, and hence they could arrest Him and hand Him over to the governor to be judged. If He agreed that taxes should be paid to Caesar, this indicated that He was endorsing the Jewish enslavement by the Romans, whereas, as the Messiah, He should have been freeing the Jews from Roman slavery.

This clearly reveals their cunningness and desire to trap Jesus in a situation where He would be condemned and rejected no matter His reply. If His reply was *yes*, He would be rejected by His followers, who expected the Messiah to free them from slavery. If His reply was *no*, He would seem to be resisting Caesar and thus could be handed over to judgment.

Christ's reply, however, astonished everyone. He requested a *denarius* and asked them, *'Whose image and inscription is this?'* Then, when they answered saying it was Caesar's image, Jesus said to them: *'Render to Caesar the things that are Caesar's, and to God the things that are God's'* (Mark 12:17).

In His reply, Jesus indicated that He basically has no interest in these matters because the things of this world—gold, silver, and the denarius—are Caesar's. As for Jesus, He seeks man's heart as the commandment states: *'My son, give me your heart, and let your eyes observe my ways'* (Proverbs 23:26).

c. The resurrection of the dead

The Sadducees, a sect of the Jews who did not believe that there is a resurrection, came to Jesus and asked Him, saying:

There was a man who married a woman and then he died without having any children. According to the Law of Moses, his brother took the woman as his wife to raise offspring for his brother. There were seven brothers. The first took her as a wife and he died; then, the second took her as a wife and he died; the third likewise, and so on until the seventh. So the seven had her as a wife and they all died without having any children. Last of all, the woman died. If You (Jesus) say that there is resurrection and all of them will be in heaven, there will be a big problem as to which of them this woman will be the wife of, since she was a wife to all seven (Mark 12:19–23).

Jesus replied saying: *'When they rise from the dead, they neither marry nor are given in marriage, but are like angels in heaven'* (Mark 12:25). Then, Jesus quoted the proof of the resurrection from the books of Moses: *'The God of Abraham, the God of Isaac, and the God of Jacob ... He is not the God of the dead, but the God of the living'* (Mark 12:26, 27).

d. Other discourses related to the state of the heart

One of the scribes asked Jesus: *'Which is the first commandment of all?'*[77]

Jesus replied:

> *The first of all the commandments is: 'Hear, O Israel, the Lord our God, the Lord is one. And you shall love the Lord your God with all your heart, with all your soul, with all your mind, and with all your strength.' This is the first commandment* (Mark 12:29, 30).

This is followed by another scene where Jesus asked a question as He taught in the temple, which surprised everyone. He asked whether Christ is the *Son of David* or *the Lord of David.*

Everyone knew that Christ is the Son of David. However, the Psalm says: *'The Lord said to my Lord'* (Psalm 110:1). Therefore, Jesus said to the people: *'Therefore David himself calls Him "Lord"; how is He then his Son?'*[78]

Christ is indeed the Son of David according to the flesh; how then can Christ be the Lord of David?

This matter was difficult to understand; therefore, no one replied to this question. Quite often, when we come across verses that are difficult to understand, like this verse, we tend to set them aside and forget about them, considering that understanding these unclear verses is a feat for scholars only, which is, of course, not true!

This episode is followed by two comments by Jesus. One is about the hypocrisy of the scribes who care about outward appearance and formalities, and the other is about putting money into the treasury (the widow's two mites) and how God looks at the heart

---

77 Mark 12:28
78 Mark 12:37

and that His assessment is different from what people see from the outside (Mark 12:38–44).

Finally, in chapter 13, there is a discourse about the second coming.

After this brief overview of Christ's discourses, we now want to understand the spiritual principles and meanings highlighted through these scenes.

In fact, these scenes are interconnected, and each scene leads to the next.

The parable of the vineyard and the vinedressers indicates that every believer ought to have fruitful work and fruitful ministry in God's Kingdom.

Since we said that the scenes lead to one another, this scene should be connected to the next one about rendering to Caesar the things that are Caesar's and to God the things that are God's. A question will thus arise: Should this fruitful work occupy all of one's time? Should one set apart all of one's time for prayer? Or should one maintain a balance between both—and if so, how can this be achieved?

The answer to this is to render to Caesar the things that are Caesar's and to God the things that are God's. The main focus of the believer should be on Jerusalem, meaning his fellowship with God and obedience to God.

One ought to have a close fellowship with God and worship God in sincerity and truth. One ought to find his true fulfillment in his fellowship with God, receive God's grace, read God's Word, understand the Kingdom principles, and then go out to his work and tend his vineyard (each according to the work he does) so that one's work may bear fruits and glorify God.

At the same time, one ought to be aware that there is a time for everything, and hence one needs to watch and be vigilant on how he spends his time in general, for the Scripture says: *'Redeeming the time, because the days are evil'* (Ephesians 5:16). The more one is vigilant and walks uprightly in spiritual matters, the more his human matters in general are set right.

This discourse is followed by the one about the resurrection of the dead. How is this scene and its spiritual significance linked to the previous scene or principle?

Naturally, when one faces the practical challenge of rendering to Caesar the things that are Caesar's and to God the things that are God's, one may first fluctuate between the two, unable to find the right balance. Therefore, being mindful of the resurrection of the dead is a constant reminder for the person not to be swallowed up by worldly cares because one's life does not end on earth, but there is indeed eternal life (resurrection of the dead), which one ought to be mindful of and live for.

In practical life, one may face situations where he wonders whether he ought to act in a certain way or say a certain word. The answer to this is to stay away from anything that may cause one to lose his eternal life.

This is followed by the discourses that focus on the disposition of the heart.

Since we have arrived at the understanding of the importance of being mindful of our eternity, meaning that we will stand before the throne and give an account of our stewardship and the things we have been entrusted with, we ought to be aware that in heaven, matters are measured and evaluated differently. In eternal life, everything is assessed based on the intent and disposition of the heart. Therefore, in this discourse, Jesus highlights that the first commandment is to *love the Lord your God with all your heart,* and the second, like it, is to *love your neighbour as yourself.* Jesus also highlights that the standard or measure of giving an offering is based on the intent and disposition of the heart and not on the monetary amount that one gives (the widow's two mites).

In some of Christ's discourses in the Gospels, for instance in Matthew 7:21–23, we find Him highlighting that even our ministry can only be measured based on the disposition of our hearts and our fellowship with God. God does not look at our deeds, even if they are ministries, preaching, or performing miracles, but rather looks at the extent of the uprightness of our hearts and the depth of our relationship with Him. This principle is clearly highlighted in this passage in Matthew 7:

> *Not everyone who says to Me, 'Lord, Lord,' shall enter the Kingdom of heaven, but he who does the will of My Father in heaven.* ***Many will say to Me in that day, 'Lord, Lord, have we not prophesied in Your name, cast out demons in Your name, and done many wonders in Your name?'*** *And then* ***I will declare to them, 'I never knew you;*** *depart from Me, you who practice lawlessness!'* (Matthew 7:21–23).

Therefore, we ought to always be mindful of this dimension that pertains to the disposition of the heart so that it may define our actions, our relationships, and even our ministries because, in the end, everything will be assessed based on this dimension. Being mindful of this dimension will also keep us watchful, vigilant, and pure during our sojourning in the world, and in true readiness for Christ's second coming.

Therefore, this scene is immediately followed by Christ's discourse about the second coming, its signs, and its association with the judgment that was about to come upon Israel [*'This generation will by no means pass away till all these things take place'* (Mark 13:30)], and the necessity of being watchful. Notice the repetition of the word *watch* in the last passage of Mark 13:

> *Take heed,* ***watch and pray****; for you do not know when the time is. It is like a man going to a far country, who left his house and gave authority to his servants, and to each his work, and commanded the doorkeeper to watch.* ***Watch therefore****, for you do not know when the master of the house is coming—in the evening, at midnight, at the crowing of the rooster, or in the morning—lest, coming suddenly, he find you sleeping.* ***And what I say to you, I say to all: Watch!*** (Mark 13:33–37).

C. The Manifestation of Redemption Through the Crucifixion and Resurrection (Mark 14–16)

The final part of the Gospel of Mark, chapters 14–16, recounts the story of the crucifixion and resurrection. We will first give an overview of the events highlighted in this part and then discuss the practical application and how to benefit from these precious acts of redemption.

▪ First: The Crucifixion

The events of the crucifixion are full of great mysteries. Do we long to enter into these mysteries?

The cross does not only signify suffering, but the cross is also a mystery; the cross is a well; the cross is salvation; the cross is love; the cross is life; and the cross is fellowship. Sometimes this fellowship cannot be expressed in words or described, especially when one enters into its manifold depths: *'He will be quiet in His love'* (Zephaniah 3:17, AMP).

What then is the way to this fellowship and these manifold mysteries of the cross?

These chapters of the Gospel of Mark about the cross highlight this path for us, but we first need to pour out our hearts in prayer, seeking the Lord and asking Him to enter us into these depths and mysteries. Pour out your heart before the Lord now and say the following prayer:

Lord, draw me close to the mysteries of Your cross, the events of crucifixion, and the spirit of these events.

Lord, please open for me the well of Your cross so that it may cleanse me, quench my thirst, revive me, and restore me to my true and redeemed humanity and honour.

May it also vindicate me when injustice is inflicted on me without needing to say anything, for the vindication of the cross is the loudest voice that no one can stop or conquer. It is a powerful voice that justifies because the judgement comes from the Crucified One. Who then can utter a word after that?!

O Lord, please enter me into the great mystery of Your cross! Amen.

How can we practically enter into this mystery?

To understand this point, we need to understand the signs of the path of the cross as highlighted in this part of the Gospel.

Signs of the path of the cross:

1. Breaking the alabaster jar versus Judas' betrayal (Mark 14:1–11)
2. The Passover: A feast of love and mystery (Mark 14:12–31)
3. Gethsemane, the oil press
4. The trials
5. Proclaiming the Messiah

1. Breaking the Alabaster Jar Versus Judas' Betrayal (Mark 14:1–11)

The Apostle intentionally recounts the story of the woman who broke the alabaster jar at Jesus' feet (Mark 14:3–9) and the story of Judas' betrayal successively (Mark 14:10–11) to highlight a contrast. While the woman—who represents those who love the Lord—was breaking the jar of her life and love to anoint Christ's body for burial, as Jesus says (Mark 14:8), Judas—who represents those who betray the Lord—was conspiring with the high priests to hand over his Master and Lord to them to be crucified.

This is how the scene is viewed from heaven, for the Lord looks at the heart. He sees hearts that love Him and hearts that betray Him. The most difficult form of betrayal comes from His own children who believe in His name or from His disciples—the ministers and pastors. What a painful scene!

Therefore, we must watch lest we find ourselves among those who betray Christ! At the same time, let us multiply our love and sacrifice for the Lord and break our alabaster jars at His feet to comfort His wounded heart that has been wounded due to the multitude of betrayals in our generation!

2. The Passover: A Feast of Love and Mystery (Mark 14:12–31)

The Lord sat with His disciples to eat the Passover. Jesus had attended the Passover feast with His disciples in previous years; however, this final Passover was different. This was because this was the Passover of salvation in which the Lord deposited His mystery as the slain Lamb—the true Passover Lamb—in the form of bread and wine so that it would always be available for His people and disciples in every place through the sacrament of the Eucharist. Therefore, whenever we draw near this mystery or sacrament, we must remember that we eat the mystery of His love and Passion—the mystery of His salvation.

Let us, therefore, be watchful over working out our salvation, and let us also be burdened with the salvation of others, for the Scripture says:

> *For as often as you eat this bread and drink this cup, you proclaim the Lord's death till He comes* (1 Corinthians 11:26).

3. The Oil Press

One of the channels or mysteries of the cross is that God may allow the person to go through pressing circumstances that may leave him confused and perplexed, making him feel that God has forsaken him. This experience is a specific divine economy which God allows for a certain time for a certain purpose. The person also then feels forsaken or, rather, rejected by people. People are often the ones who are quick to forsake!

Being in this situation causes the person to be confused and perplexed, wondering whether he has sinned, angered God, or caused people to stumble! In this state and these circumstances, the enemy finds a ripe atmosphere and opportunity to destroy and devastate the person. God allows this to an extent and a limit that is fully under His control to help the person work out his salvation. Therefore, as the person goes through this experience, he is truly pressed. However, this experience leads the person to the greatest lesson and blessing, to the greatest fruit, and to the greatest grace of being able to say: 'Not my will, but Your will, Lord'.

When one learns to live according to this principle, he becomes truly free from the ego, his own views, people's opinions, and the circumstances that surround him, whether easy or difficult, because his heart constantly says, 'Not my will, but Your will ... whatever You want Lord'.

4. The Trials

This includes the two main trials which the Lord faced: the religious and the civil. Both trials involved much mockery, ridicule, reproach, scourging, and all kinds of suffering that a human could go through. This means that no matter what we experience or go through, we cannot say it is beyond our ability to bear, because the Lord has already been through it all for our sake. Sometimes, He allows us to partake in some of this suffering with Him.

We may say He is the Lord while we are poor and weak humans. However, the truth is that the Lord went through all this so that if we face similar situations, instead of feeling helpless, defeated, and shaken, we can lift our hearts and eyes to Him and receive from Him not only His help but also victory over these situations.

What is it that bothers us the most when we are exposed to mockery and ridicule? Do we get offended because we seek honour from people? The honour that Christ bestows upon His children who are reproached and ridiculed for His sake heals and allows the Spirit of glory to rest upon them. The Scripture says:

> *If you are reproached for the name of Christ, blessed are you, for* ***the Spirit of glory and of God rests upon you****. On their part He is blasphemed, but on your part He is glorified* (1 Peter 4:14).

The honour and glory that the Lord grants are completely different from those offered by people. When we experience the flavor of what the Lord offers us, we will discern the difference between dust and gold, between what people offer us and what the Lord offers us.

Our insight will also be opened and we will discern that there are different kinds of human beings. Some are dust and some are gold, meaning some are genuine and some are false and deceitful.

As we go through this experience of suffering and partaking of Christ's suffering, we will also see Christ on the day of His crucifixion, and we will see the different attitudes of His disciples on that day. Some betray Him, some run away and leave Him, and some stay close to Him.

The stories of the Gospels highlight how due to our human weakness, we betray Christ. Our betrayal causes the greatest and deepest wound to His heart. But all praise and glory be to our God, for He has provided a solution even for this shameful act of betrayal. If we repent, the divine wound is healed, and we are restored to Him and to our calling!

Peter healed the wound caused by his betrayal of the Lord because he repented, while Judas did not. Judas hung himself, whereas Peter was restored to honour and to his commission, as we read in John 21, how Jesus commissioned him to feed His lambs and tend His sheep.

5. *Proclaiming the Messiah*

This proclamation is apparent in the words of Jesus about Himself, when the high priest asked if He was *'the Christ, the Son of the Blessed'*:[79]

> *I am. And you will see the Son of Man sitting at the right hand of the Power, and coming with the clouds of heaven* (Mark 14:62).

This proclamation explains the meaning of the phrase, *'My hour has not yet come'*,[80] which Jesus said on more than one occasion

79 Mark 14:61
80 John 2:4

but was hardly understood. This phrase refers to the hour of Christ's proclamation and manifestation as the Messiah. This hour[81] came on the great day of the crucifixion. Christ's proclamation as the Messiah was through His death so that He might complete our salvation and redemption. No one had expected the manifestation of the Messiah to happen in this manner.

Since His proclamation and manifestation as the Messiah meant His death on the cross for the sake of our salvation, Christ could not reveal Himself at the beginning of His ministry so that He could complete His ministry and mission on earth, and allow humanity to see how He lived and served, and witness all that was to be written about Him in the Gospels.

Then, when this mission was completed, the hour came for Him to proclaim His Messianic calling and accept crucifixion. Thus, He died and hence made us alive (meaning resurrection).

▪ Second: The Resurrection

The three main signs of the resurrection as highlighted in this part of the Gospel of Mark (Mark 16):

1. Rising Up Early in the Morning

Very early in the morning, *on the first day of the week, they came to the tomb when the sun had risen* (Mark 16:2).

This characteristic or principle is apparent in what the Marys did. They went to the tomb *very early in the morning.*

When we apply this principle to every aspect of our spiritual life, including our worship, our quick obedience to God, and living

---

81 John 12:23, 27; 17:1

a sacrificial life in our ministries, for God's sake, the mystery of His resurrection works in us!

2. *Faith*

> *And when they heard that He was alive and had been seen by her, they* ***did not believe*** *... And they went and told it to the rest, but they* ***did not believe*** *them either. Later He appeared to the eleven as they sat at the table; and He rebuked their* ***unbelief*** *and hardness of heart, because they* ***did not believe*** *those who had seen Him after He had risen* (Mark 16:11, 13, 14).

The disciples suffered from a lack of faith; therefore, they were not granted to proclaim the good news of Christ's resurrection. They were supposed to proclaim His resurrection since they had been His disciples, but this did not happen due to their lack of faith. Mary Magdalene and the other Mary[82] were the ones who proclaimed the good news of Christ's resurrection. In other words, Mary Magdalene, who had been possessed by seven demons, and the other Mary—the *weak* vessels—were the ones who proclaimed the news of *power*, for the resurrection is power. Meanwhile, the disciples, who accompanied Jesus throughout all the years of His ministry, failed to do so due to their lack of faith.

From this, we understand that the absence of faith means the absence of resurrection. If resurrection is absent, this, in turn, implies the absence of life. It also indicates that the person has not experienced Christ's complete salvation because Christ's salvation is complete by His resurrection. Consequently, if one knows Christ only as the Crucified One, this means that this

82 The Three Marys (also spelled Maries) are women mentioned in the canonical Gospels' narratives of the crucifixion and resurrection of Jesus. All four Gospels mention women going to the tomb of Jesus, but only Mark 16:1 mentions the three that this tradition interprets as bearing the name Mary: Mary Magdalene, Mary of Clopas, Mary Salome.

person has not yet experienced coming out of the tomb with Christ and tasting the power and life of His resurrection!

Based on this, we can see that faith is essential as it allows the person to experience the fullness of the manifestation of Christ's complete redemption, which includes the acts of crucifixion and resurrection together:

> *He was delivered over to death for our sins and was raised to life for our justification* (Romans 4:25, NIV).

> *Moreover, brethren, I declare to you the gospel which I preached to you, which also you received and in which you stand, by which also you are saved, if you hold fast that word which I preached to you—unless you believed in vain. For I delivered to you first of all that which I also received: that Christ died for our sins according to the Scriptures, and that He was buried, and that He rose again the third day according to the Scriptures,* (1 Corinthians 15:1–4).

3. *The Great Commission and the Companionship of the Lord*

> *And He said to them, "Go into all the world and preach the gospel to every creature"... And they went out and preached everywhere, the Lord working with them and confirming the word through the accompanying signs. Amen* (Mark 16:15, 20).

After His resurrection, the Lord sent forth His disciples, accompanied them, and worked with them. This companionship of the Lord and His sending forth of His disciples, and His children in general, is another channel of resurrection.

To sum up this part, the cross and the resurrection are wells of salvation. Each of these wells has its specific channels, which God allows us to go through to receive more from these wells of salvation. However, we unfortunately often go through these channels without understanding their purpose and hence do not benefit fully from them.

For instance, God may allow a person to go through the *oil press* in order to teach him to surrender his will, not a passive surrender but a victorious and trusting surrender. The person may not understand why he is going through these difficult situations; thus, he may cry out, rebel, and grumble. Because God is a tender and loving Father, He cannot bear to see the person in this state of suffering and struggling, hence He stops this plan of His salvific economy for the person, since the person cannot bear it or respond to it. As a result, the person will have gone through this experience and come out of it without fulfilling God's purpose and plan for this experience, which was to help the person deal with his rebellious and unsubmissive will and mind. Consequently, the person's will will remain rebellious and unsubmissive and his mind and thoughts not completely surrendered to the Lord. Therefore, this person will not be able to say from his heart that everything is in God's hands and that everything will work for his good, as the Scripture says in Romans 8:28. He will not be able to say that no one nor anything, neither human beings nor demons, can control his life, for God alone is in control of his life, as Apostle Paul teaches us, saying:

> *For I am persuaded that neither death nor life, nor angels nor principalities nor powers, nor things present nor things to come, nor height nor depth, nor any other created thing, shall be able to separate us from the love of God which is in Christ Jesus our Lord* (Romans 8:38, 39).

This is indeed the path that leads the person to wholeheartedly say, 'Not my will, but Your will,' or say as Apostle Paul said when Jesus appeared to him on his way to Damascus: *'Lord, what do You want me to do?'* (Acts 9:6).

This is one example of the channels of the cross and the importance of understanding these channels and understanding their work in order to benefit from them.

The resurrection also has its channels, as we highlighted. Therefore, if one truly desires to enter into the rich well of resurrection and allow it to open up for him so that the power, life, and mysteries of the resurrection may be poured out from this well, one needs to learn these channels. One of these channels, as highlighted earlier, is rising up early in the morning to pray. Is the act of rising up early to pray an act of the spirit or the body? It is, of course, an act done by the body because it is the body that wakes up early and not the spirit. However, when the body learns to rise up early, the heart will in turn learn to be early, meaning it will hasten towards God and hasten to obey Him and be quick and early in its obedience, as Isaiah said: *'Here am I! Send me'* (Isaiah 6:8).

Every step of wakefulness and watchfulness that one takes leads to another degree of watchfulness and wakefulness through the work of the resurrection, and it qualifies the person to receive a new grace from the well of resurrection. Therefore, the resurrection grants us watchfulness and wakefulness of the body, mind, heart, and spirit!

The same applies to *faith*, which is the second channel of the well of resurrection, as we said earlier. God searches for those who trust in Him so that when He commissions them with tasks in His Kingdom, He is reassured that they will carry out these tasks and will not allow their hearts to slumber due to a lack of watchfulness and prayer.[83]

If the heart slumbers, the person consequently begins to fluctuate between faith and the lack of faith. This fluctuation is serious and

83 Matthew 26:41

dangerous; therefore, we ought to take heed because when we have faith, we are in God's sphere and protection, but when we lose our faith, we come out of God's sphere and enter into the enemy's sphere. As a result, the work of God's Kingdom with which we have been entrusted may be ruined. Therefore, the Lord seeks those whom He can trust and those who will be steadfast in their faith in order to entrust them with His Kingdom work and send them forth.

These are the signs that the Gospel outlines and highlights for us to follow. We cannot live a spiritual life that grows, shines, and glorifies God unless we live it out according to the biblical measures and standards. This is available for us insofar as we have a living relationship with the Word of God, reading it unceasingly, perceiving it in our spirits, receiving its light and illumination, and fully obeying it. Thus, it truly becomes a source of fullness and joy for us, as the Scripture says:

> *Your words were found, and I ate them, and Your word was to me the joy and rejoicing of my heart; for I am called by Your name, O Lord God of hosts* (Jeremiah 15:16).

> *Your word is a lamp to my feet and a light to my path* (Psalm 119:105).

Finally, I want to conclude this study by quoting the closing passage of this Holy Gospel:

> *Later He appeared to the eleven as they sat at the table; and He rebuked their unbelief and hardness of heart, because they did not believe those who had seen Him after He had risen. And He said to them, "Go into all the world and preach the gospel to every creature. He who believes and is baptised will be saved; but he who does not believe will be condemned. And these signs will follow those who believe: In My name they will cast out demons; they*

will speak with new tongues; they will take up serpents; and if they drink anything deadly, it will by no means hurt them; they will lay hands on the sick, and they will recover." So then, after the Lord had spoken to them, He was received up into heaven, and sat down at the right hand of God. And they went out and preached everywhere, the Lord working with them and confirming the word through the accompanying signs. Amen (Mark 16:14–20).

Glory be to God forever.

Made in the USA
Coppell, TX
27 May 2026

77838576R00121